CW00499919

The Tracks of my Tyres - a Life

For my generation cars were a rite of passage and I can chart much of my life through the cars I have owned and my time spent in them which is not insignificant. Previous generations such as my parents were the first generation where car ownership became almost universal but that change also happened within my lifetime. Certainly when I was in school it wasn't always the case that school friends owned a car in their family so often weekend outings in our early family cars may have been accompanied by friends from families without a car. The writings document the cars I have owned through my life and my experiences with them. Some of them are funny in retrospect but maybe less so at the time. Maybe some of the experiences are mundane but this lays no claim to be the memoirs of a formula 1 racing driver (those are available I am sure.)
Instead they are a series of anecdotes that may strike chords among readers from their own experiences with the horseless carriage that has come to dominate our lives and times.
I apologise in advance for any technical inaccuracies that will be down to a mixture of amnesia, ignorance and antipathy to accuracy.
My own first car was a child's metal pedal car which I soon grew out and it was passed on to my younger brother although in any event the small size of our childhood garden limited the attraction of this early venture into the world of motoring.

In childhood model cars were an important and the ownership of a scale model garage with a lift, ramp and a showroom behind a curved perspex window was an early introduction to

the enticing world of car dealerships. In recent years I have started a small collection of miniatures of some of the cars I have owned and photos of these appear as an appendix.
I am aware that driving is becoming less popular among subsequent generations particularly city dwellers. A number of factors are apparently influencing this ranging from environmental concerns to the cost of lessons - who knows, maybe they are waiting for self-driving flying cars from Elon Musk.
Before I passed my driving test I experienced a false entry into the world of motorised two wheels with the acquisition of a Vespa scooter. For the princely sum I think of £15 I acquired a ten year old metallic blue scooter. Although initially pleased with it ownership was not a happy experience. The only mechanical transport that I have owned that was less reliable was a four wheel ride-on-lawn mower many years later. I spent more time maintaining it than cutting grass with it. Other friends also had bikes and scooters of mixed reliability. The main problem with mine was an troublesome cable change for the gears and I can remember a number of slow returns home with the gearbox stuck in first or second gear. We lived up a hill at the time so the alternative of pushing it home was not an attractive one. Unlike a number of my friends I don't remember any accidents on it. Maybe it wasn't mobile often enough for them to occur. I didn't take my motorbike test so was unable to graduate to larger engined motorbikes which was probably just

as well, if I am going to experience rapid acceleration I would prefer it to be on four wheels wearing a seatbelt.
Once I passed my driving test I left the world of two wheels with no real reluctance.
A couple of my school friends had taken and passed their driving tests before I had and this being the 1960's the cars they drove, nominally owned by their mothers, were Mini's and when I did take a few driving lessons and entered for my test it was also in a Mini. Compared to the cars of today and particularly the 21st century BMW Mini they were cars of a different complexion. The first difference was their size - they looked tiny and low to the ground with very small wheels pushed out to the four corners. Inside they seemed implausibly to have more space than you would think from the outside. Some of this space was achieved by pushing the inside close to the outside, that is neglecting any thick insulation panels on the doors, boot and panels. The lowness and lack of sound deadening allowed a greater sensation of speed amplified by the noise of the engine that sounded as if it was in the passenger compartment with you. This was described as giving a sporting characteristic an impression confirmed to owners by the success of the cars in rallying including winning the famous Monte Carlo rally. They would ignore the fact that the rally winner was a Mini Cooper S that had been tuned by a team of rally mechanics - this was an inconvenience - so in a world yet to be subjected to airbags, seat belt

laws and breathalysers, Minis were often driven as if in rallies. This was particularly true of my school friends in their mother's Minis. I remember returning in a following car from an outing to a country pub near Llandeilo to spot a friend's car sitting on a lawn of a bungalow on a tight bend, facing towards the road and the occupants clambering out to be harangued by the resident over the recently created gap in his hedge caused by the Mini losing control and spinning off the road. I think it was pushed back through the hedge and driven back home!

My driving lessons were in a Mini but additional practice was in my father's car, a Hillman Imp. This was a rival to the Mini and a less common car but innovative in different ways. Firstly the engine was in the back which tended to make the front lighter and affected the steering handling because of this set up. There was talk of putting a paving slab in the front luggage compartment to improve handling although I don't remember my Dad resorting to this. There was synchromesh on all four gears which was radical having been described as impossible by Sir Alec Issigonis the designer of the Mini and this made it easier to engage first gear at junctions.
There was a hatchback window at the rear and the backseat folded down for load carrying, (maybe useful if you had filled your front boot with paving slabs!) The engine was aluminium making it lighter and featured an overhead camshaft. All these made it different from the

ubiquitous and rather more successful Mini and personally made it difficult to transition between the two cars while learning to drive. Nevertheless I passed my test at the first attempt and can still remember the eerie sense of freedom being in my Dad's car by myself. In those days in-car entertainment was mostly limited to your own singing and the intrusive noise of the car engine and road noise plus any sounds your passengers might make. I was able to experience this first hand shortly after passing my test when my Dad was foolish or kind enough, depending on your perspective to let me borrow the Imp one evening. I collected a couple of friends, I believe beer was drunk and an attempt was made to settle an argument caused by an article in the motoring press that a Hillman Imp was capable of 70 miles per hour in third gear, whilst a Mini

wasn't. Driving on the nearest dual carriageway out of Swansea the little blue car was wound up to the mid 60's mph in third but seemed reluctant to edge the speedometer needle beyond the 70 mark.
One of our number suggested changing up to fourth gear exceeding the 70 mark and changing gear down into third and see if that worked. The effect did indeed show 70 mph, briefly, in third before the combined effect of the car lurching, the engine and the car's occupants screaming in unison meant the experiment whilst arguably successful was short lived and never, ever, to be repeated. We drove home sedately watching the car's temperature gauge hovering near the red mark. My father when he welcomed me back onto the drive at home thought the engine smelled hot and remarked that he must check the water and oil levels as he couldn't remember when he had last done that. This photo of an Imp's interior shows the speedometer, a horizontal instrument, with strange dash mounted stalks for indicators and wipers I think.

The descriptions that follow about my own cars will not be a technical list of details that

would be of interest to automotive enthusiasts but rather my own take on the cars, their idiosyncrasies and the adventures and mishaps I enjoyed during their ownership. There will be an ability to vaguely trace car design and innovation over the decades with a number of examples of improvements that were viewed as luxuries or major advances at the time to soon become essentials and mainstream.

My Austin A35

My own first car, an Austin A 35 was less technically advanced than the Hillman Imp but nevertheless provided a more independent way of getting to my second year of university.The car was a very old fashioned design produced between 1956 and 1959 a rounded, friendly bodywork shape the front of which is recognisable as a van version is used in the Wallace and Gromit films as the bakery van. The A35 was quite old fashioned looking and I was mildly jealous of my university friend, Cledwyn who owned the much more modern looking A40, more angular and with an early hatchback rear door.
Though this envy was tempered by a stronger jealousy of another friend's Triumph Spitfire

which seemed the last word in style and sophistication. So thanks Mike for sowing the seed in my mind that may have led me to eventually own one a few years later.

I believe my A35 was from 1958 and I owned it in 1971. It had some 'refinements' - the bonnet had been replaced with one from another car. The car was black whilst the bonnet was grey and wasn't entirely fitted properly so was held down with two leather straps and buckles. This was apparently common in earlier sports cars such as 1930's blower Bentleys with which other racing features mine did not share. Strangely whilst researching and writing for this book I came across a photo of one of my Dad's early cars from my childhood which was a grey Austin A30 - could the bonnet have been a later transplant donation onto my black A35 and hence the poor fitting - spooky!
It did have a feature similar to James Bond's Aston Martin in the form of a sort of ejector seat. The passenger seat wasn't consistently secured to the floor so that occasionally when in motion and perhaps the result of over exuberant 'racing' gear changes the front fixings would release pivoting the whole seat and the passenger backwards - like Bond's ejector seat. I would have preferred the front facing machine guns but you can't have everything.
Reading a motoring web site specification of the model they extol the virtues of flashing indicator bulb over the previous A30 model's indicator arms which on many earlier cars popped up out of the side of the car to indicate

turning - quaint really. This exciting development must have not been fully debugged on my car as the dashboard switch for this had been replaced with a cheap metal toggle switch which not only didn't self cancel but didn't flash to tell me when they were on and I am sure I spent a large proportion of my journeys flashing the last direction of turn for a number of miles making for a certain amount of confusion amongst fellow road users.

Many car designers in the quest for greater speed go to great lengths to reduce the weight of their cars and also reduce air resistance by removing unnecessary projections and protuberances. I accidentally achieved this one night when my rear bumper became unfixed at one end and alerted me to the mishap by a loud scraping noise in the rear and a cloud of sparks visible in the rear view mirror. Pulling over I found it was securely fastened on the side where it was still attached so it came away with a quick tug. I found it just fitted in the boot where it stayed for a few weeks with the car enjoying the new streamlined look while not actually gaining any weight reduction. It transpired that not opting for the weight reduction option by leaving the number at home was to prove beneficial. Several weeks later I was pulled over by the police late one night and having checked my driving licence and established the tyres weren't bald and the car's lights were all functioning, including the non-cancelling indicators the officer was jubilant to notice the missing rear bumper. "Where's your rear bumper?" - I responded by opening the boot to show him. In fairness to him I could see he was doing his best not to laugh so to my relief his muttered. "Get off home and have it fixed tomorrow was a satisfactory end to the matter.

Sadly this was not the most dramatic event in my car although miraculously I never had an accident in it despite driving it as fast as the tiny engine would allow it. No the drama was provided by the car itself attempting to convert itself into a three wheeler which was a popular design for cheap cars at the time. I never owned one until one afternoon driving in Gower when the car just didn't feel right rounding a bend and as I drove into the next bend on the road crossing Clyne Common the car felt a whole lot stranger as simultaneously the car lurched to the left and dropped in height accompanied by a terrible grinding noise and I spotted a wheel heading down the road in front of me before the realisation dawned that this may well be one of the wheels previously attached to the car.

The two following cars driven by friends came to a halt having managed to drive round me when I had 'ground to a halt.' There was a long scrape on the road surface and thankfully there didn't seem to be any fluids leaking out from under the car. One friend arrived back rolling the errant wheel and cheerfully told me the wheel nuts were still inside held in place by the hubcap. Another friend optimistically told me that the threads on the hub looked ok and hadn't been stripped so the wheel should go back on. Between the three cars we had two car jacks, both of the flimsy scissor type and not suitable to raise the car from it's lowly position. A garage was known to be a short way up the road so an expedition was sent off to borrow a trolley jack. This being post 1960's, and as a group there was an air of Led Zeppelins' roadies about us, the garage owner demanded security that was provided by leaving a watch with them. The trolley jack did the trick, the wheel was put back on, my then girlfriend was reassured by all that the car would be perfectly safe and so she somewhat reluctantly got back in. She was entitled to a certain amount of caution as she had recently experienced the ejector seat feature on a previous outing. After a short debate as to whether the watch would be a fair swap for the trolley jack it was returned to the garage and we all drove somewhere for a reviving coffee. Fortunately the car remained a four wheeler for the rest of my ownership.

During my experience of cars either as passenger or a driver reliability has improved by a huge margin. There is no better example of this than the seconds before driving off. In my early cars there was always the air of anticipation when turning the key to start the engine - would it fire, was there even enough electricity in the battery to fire the starting motor to turn the engine?

There were always particular routines required - some recommended a quick depression of the accelerator to prime the fuel. There was usually in older cars a choke lever to pull out which temporarily restricted air flow to the carburettor and which you had to remember to push back in once the engine was warmer. If these routines didn't work in post war cars there was the option of the manual starter handle. This was a form of hand crank inserted into the front of the car and allowed the car engine to be 'turned over' to start. That is if the person winding the handle was strong enough and usually required sychronising with someone sitting in the car performing the aforementioned pedal depression or choke operation and if unsuccessful this person was usually accused of 'flooding' the engine by the red faced and sweating operator of the winding handle. It was not usually a happy operation. More fun could be had with cars without a hand cranking option by 'bump-starting' the car. This requires one of more willing helpers to push the car while the driver inside having put the car in neutral gear and released the handbrake turns on the ignition and makes a judgement at a point when the car has achieved sufficient speed to start when one of the forward gears are engaged. Potential problems are to employ a car related term - manifold.

Firstly there is likely to be accusations thrown by the breathless helpers pushing at the driver sitting in the car that the handbrake is not completely released, the ignition is not on or the wrong gear has been selected - hopefully not reverse as this would turn mere frustration into potential disaster if the car started. Again there are the same potential pitfalls of choke or flooding errors. Even if the car is successful in starting at best the pushers are usually enveloped in a smelly and smoky cloud of exhaust gas as the car engine suddenly bursts into life. Of course they may be unfortunate to have avoided this by the unsatisfactory tactic of being so surprised at the car starting and lurching forward away from them that they end up face down and prone in the road. Neither option is ideal and I am sorry to say that I have witnessed and participated in both scenarios.

For almost a whole half term at university my A35 gave me multiple opportunities to witness and practice these as the starter motor failed and I either couldn't get a replacement or more likely I temporarily didn't have the funds to replace it. My student flat was at the top of a steep hill in Aberystwyth with the shops, friends and much social life on the level near the sea front. Leaving the flat wasn't so difficult but i often had to bribe friends with a free ride back up to the campus providing they participated in the 'bump start' exercise. I also can claim to have performed the procedure 'solo' - quite an act of derring do as it required a quiet, wide road, ideally sloping downhill and after a shove from outside the drivers open door you had to leap into the car and perform

the ignition, choke, throttle, gear engagement routine whilst steering it back on a straight course. I got quite adept at it and was told it had entertainment value as a spectacle.
Another method of starting was through the use of jump leads - a set of heavy duty cables, usually one red and one black with a large set of sprung clamps known for obvious reasons as crocodile clips at either end. You would connect your car engine to a 'donor' car's electrical system and while their engine was running you would use their electrics to power your starter.
As students you first had to find someone else's car that started reliability, the required set of jump leads, correct connections and the madness to muck about with cables under the bonnet of a car with the engine running - assuming it started. There was also the added excitement of generating electrical sparks in an engine bay likely to harbour escaped petrol fumes and a reasonable number of oily surfaces. Life had its excitement and random dangers in those days.
In a modern car this is not often performed as its not usually required but if it is the required connections are usually masked by plastic shrouding that disguises the component engine parts.

I can't find any photos of my Austin A35 despite being very proud of it at the time but this is my Dad's A30 which is very similar in appearance.

Roadside repairs were quite a commonplace event in those days and the combination of the relative simplicity of cars of that time, the optimism of youth coupled with the lack of funds for more professional help all served to help with this. I recall two events performed on my father's cars, one without his knowledge and one with. His Hillman Imp was lent to me occasionally and on one such loan on a run with friends to a Gower beach the car refused to move. I believe we had stopped at Shepherd's in Parkmill to buy food and drink for a picnic. When attempting to pull away not only didn't the car move but the inertia was accompanied by a loud clanking noise from underneath the

rear of the car. Getting out and crawling underneath revealed some large kind of octagonal rubber doughnut split in two that was the link between the drive shaft and the rear wheel. Checking the other side revealed it should indeed be one whole piece. Youthful optimism suggested that if a replacement could be obtained the repair would be possible. A call from the nearby phone box to a spares garage in Swansea located the required part and could be collected from them, (those were the days - phone boxes and copies of the Yellow Pages - no smart phones and Google searches.)
An hour later my friend Geoff arrived back with the 'rubber doughnut' part and a toolkit. Amazingly the nuts and bolts holding the old part on were removed relatively easily, the new part fitted and the beach picnic resumed. My father was never told about the repair and our mechanical knowledge had marginally been extended. This knowledge was rashly employed a few years later when after leaving university I was back at home waiting to start my first proper job as a graduate trainee with a power company in the south east of England. One day my father announced that the engine in his Ford Cortina had a broken piston ring and had seized while emerging from the garage at home. Having time on my hands and full of youthful bravado I announced that I was sure we could replace the rings and repair it at home. As my Dad was working full-time the 'we' mostly meant me so armed with the appropriate Haynes manual, a borrowed socket

set and a large tin of Swarfega (a luminous green, jelly like de-greaser for cleaning your hands.) Although I had never attempted anything so ambitious mechanically I was sure it was possible and also felt this would be a useful start to my career in the engineering sector although thankfully my role was to be in an administrative function and safely away from the operation of the power network. I have to say despite a long career I never fully understood the product or even how the electricity stays in the wall when there's no plug in the socket!

After several greasy days in the garage with the car and many cups of coffee and hours of radio I somehow managed to remove the old piston rings and install all new ones in the four cylinders and reinstall them in the engine block. The triumph was short lived as despite several attempts the engine would not turn over or start. Some days later I was relieved to hear when phoning home from my new job in Kent that my Dad and a friend had bump started the car by towing it and after a bang and a roar the engine was running fine as they proved sometime later by visiting me in Folkestone. Wisely I refrained from offering any mechanical expertise in my new career.

Not long after entering the world of permanent employment I decided that I should re-enter the world of car ownership. This had come to an abrupt end while at university when a failed MOT on multiple issues meant I sold the A35 for scrap after a years ownership.

Triumph Herald

My new car was an upgrade and at the time considered quite stylish - a gunmetal blue 1966 Triumph Herald 12/50. I was told the 12 referred to a 1200 cc engine and the 50 was the mighty 50 horse power it produced. It had a wooden dashboard, blue vinyl seats (with white piping!), a sliding vinyl sun roof, two doors, white rubber bumpers and a pair of fins at the back like a mini Cadillac. Did it have a radio? I really can't remember but the well secured and comfortable seats, a bonnet that fitted and two bumpers did seem some progress. I have since discovered it was fitted with front disc brakes which I had forgotten but I do remember it having a very tight turning circle

which allowed you to do U-turns in one go in a normal road width, like London cab, (but without the non-stop opinionated commentary!) Despite my pride owning this marvel of British engineering
I only seem to posses three photos of it. I recall it boasted a fair amount of chrome that needed cleaning and was light inside because of the large windows. Also that the front bonnet and wings all swung forward in one piece to give good access to the engine which could be sometimes 'attended to' whilst sitting on one of the front tyres which seemed a benefit in those days of home mechanical repairs. I can remember cleaning out the carburettor, changing the plugs and filters and at one MOT test I was informed the 'trunnion bushes' needed replacing. First of all I was unaware I possessed trunnion bushes and was ignorant of where they were and what they were for. I think the repair wasn't too expensive and it hasn't happened in any other car so I hope it's not a skyhook type of scam for garages. Now it sound like something Heston Blumenthal would include in one of his recipes. The car did have one fault which was an irritatingly loud vibration noise which would emanate from the gear lever. I found that if I held the gear lever and steered with one hand it reduced the noise considerably. On longer journeys such as a trip down the M4 from Kent to Wales I would tension the lever by a hooked rubber elasticated-gungie and attach the other end underneath the drivers seat. This required rapid release at

the toll services on the Severn bridge but satisfactorily suppressed the noise. Happily back in Folkestone the son of a neighbour who also owned a Triumph explained he had solved the problem with a set of replacement bearings and bushes available from Triumph spares. He also told me (which I already suspected,) that the gungie treatment was only aggravating the problem. One evening he helped me dismantle the gear lever and we solved the problem at least temporarily. I think that for the next couple of years I repeated the repair. There was either something wrong with the gear stick or the way was changing gear. I have a vague memory of this suspicion being confirmed when a particularly aggressive gear change on a hill out of Dover left me holding the gearstick which had separated from the rest of the car. The lesson from this is that reassembly needs as much attention as disassembly - maybe more !

Around this time I was to experience one of what I call my 'Toad of Toad Hall' moments. In the Wind in the Willows Toad is rendered speechless when he witnessed a speeding car and can only say 'poop, poop,' until he acquires his own roadster. Mine was on the sea front road between Folkestone and Hythe when I spotted a vision in metallic blue, chrome and glass; a low sleek two seater fixed roof sports car. I discovered it was a Volvo 1800 ES and it was another twenty five years or so before I was to acquire a 1973 ES one of my own. It still looked fantastic but was a bit of a pig to drive but more of that story later.

Going Italian - Fiat 127

My next car was to be more modern which wasn't too difficult as the Austin had dated from 1958 and the Triumph was already six or seven years old when I bought it but this was a common pattern of car ownership amongst people of my age at the time. The new car a mere two years old was a further stride into later 20th century technology. Quite what modern advances this new limousine possessed I am struggling to remember but coming clean it was a Fiat 127 hatchback improbably described as an early supermini. Again it was two doors but with a hatchback and a flat folding rear seat. An 903 cc engine was mounted transversally and described in Wikipedia as state of the art at that time!

It felt quite sporty but I think this was an impression gained from its exhaust note that I would think was based on the Vespa scooter. My research reveals it won the European car of the year award and sold over one million units within three years of its launch. Compared to the A35, Triumph Herald and even the Mini the Fiat at least looked like it might have been tried in a wind tunnel before the design was finalised. Trying to remember any standout features has left me a little stumped. The hatchback and fold flat seats was certainly useful as I was involved in 'do- it-yourself' and decorating our house in common with most twenty somethings at that time and flat pack furniture was now available. The rear window had an electric demisting element, there were hazard warning lights and I think there was a radio but I might have put that in. Despite the relative spartan features it proved reliable so much so that I believe it's the car out of all those I have owned that was driven furthest from home. Travelling to the South of France and into Spain on some scary roads over the Pyrenees this fact alone gives it some kudos. I recall that that journey required tinting the headlights amber, installing a map reading light and a green sun screen strip on the windscreen as well as buying a folding warning triangle. It was my first experience of driving on the wrong side of the road, at least intentionally, and the journey around Paris's Peripherique ring road was quite memorable and a white knuckle ride.

I also had an accident in this, thankfully a minor one, skidding on ice in the office car park and incurring minor damage to a wing hitting a wall. Anyone who has experienced aquaplaning or skidding on ice will remember the experience as particularly unnerving - the silence, lack of control and the long seconds waiting for a possible impact - not nice, and it made me very cautious of icy roads. Modern cars now often show a little snowflake warning in the instruments if the temperature is down to 4 degrees C and I welcome this.

Triumph Spitfire

My next car was viewed by me as a further leap up the ladder of cool despite it being an older car and design.

It was a red sports car! Too young to have a mid-life crisis and still possessing a full head of hair I succumbed to the dubious pleasures (at least in the UK,) of open topped motoring. The car in question was a 1970 mark 3 Triumph Spitfire with a 1300 cc engine complete with twin carburettors, (whatever happened to them?) and a fold down hood. Bought from the original one owner, a family member by marriage it was in good original condition and had been well looked after. Although the published performance figures (13 seconds 0 - 60 and a top speed of 95 mph) are pedestrian compared to modern cars the wind in the hair, the noise and low seating position near the ground gave it an enhanced sensation of speed. In this car I experience seeing my first 100 mph on the speedometer.

The car also was fitted with a radio and 8 track tape stereo and I am sure the introduction of loud rock music into the car enhanced the driving style. The size of the 8 track cassettes, almost the size of VHS tapes or small paperback book to those readers mystified by VHS tape references, and limited storage space in the car meant the same tapes were played over and over. I can only recall a Santana album, a Dylan one, Blood Sweat and Tears and a Them album featuring a young Van Morrison.

I eventually replaced the 8 track with a radio cassette player that allowed playing a greater range of music through the 1970's popularity of home taping. People would loan their records to each other and copy them onto tape cassettes. I am sure working musicians might see this as the start of the erosion of musicians earnings ending up with iTunes and Spotify. The Spitfire shared some similarities with my previous Triumph Herald including the folding out of the whole wings and bonnet allowing easy engine access. As I said earlier this was the era of home mechanics out of enthusiasm or economy or both. It was probably one of the last cars that I performed extensive maintenance on with routine tasks such as cleaning carburettors, adjusting the ignition and replacing plugs and filters as well as brake parts and exhausts. I believe that the Spitfire also required the occasional replacement of bushes and washers in the gear change which I could now execute, if not blindfold, certainly easily. I even fitted an electronic ignition unit that avoided the regular chore of adjusting the ignition points. Car home mechanics magazines were quite popular and helpful work colleagues would tear out a relevant article for your car. Through this medium I learnt how to balance the twin carbs and set ignition timings. There were other 'improvements,' although some of these were more dubious in their inherent advantages. The first of these made me realise why it was fashionable for some cars to have small red cylindrical fire extinguisher in the car.

I had always thought these to be an affectation but one had come with the car clamped to the transmission tunnel in the passenger footwell. I had for some time anticipated a fidgety passenger accidentally setting it off with their feet and filling the small interior with a mass of foam. In the event when I needed to use it it took so long to undo the clips and the nozzle the potential danger had subsided.

It was all my own fault. The car along with most of that era wasn't equipped with rear fog lights. A helpful article in 'Maniac Mechanic' or some such publication suggested the keen owner with some small black box and some cable clips could adapt the circuitry to the rear brake lights to partially brighten them to an intermediate brightness between normal rear lights and full brake lights. I duly installed it with a new switch boasting a red warning bulb into a spare position on the dashboard. For some weeks all was well until one morning, driving up Reigate hill heading for the office in south London, I encountered thick fog. Rather smugly I threw the switch and all was well, briefly, until I was aware that as well as a lack of visibility outside the car was accompanied by a growing fogginess inside the car which I soon realised was acrid smelling smoke. Luckily I pulled over praying that nobody was going to rear end me. Switching off the ignition and taking out the fire extinguisher I prepared to tackle a conflagration. To my relief it seems that switching off the ignition had stopped the fire. Getting back in and looking for the source

of the potential disaster I soon found that my new 'improvement' was the source and the smoke was the melting of the insulation on the newly installed wires. Disconnecting this I was relieved to find there was no further damage and the lights and brake lights still functioned. I returned the magazine cutting to me work colleague and suggested politely where he could put it.

They say you learn by your mistakes but I am not sure this is always universally true as some of us bravely and doggedly pursue the search for excellence and new life experiences. Probably in one of the mechanical magazines that I should now be studiously ignoring after the brake light fire there were instructions for improving your windscreen washers. The improvements were to convert the normal boring cold water wash to a HOT wash, infinitely more effective for the removal of road grime, salt and dead flies. The instructions were simple and to my mind ingenious. You were to insert in the section of hose from the reservoir to the windscreen jets an additional length of thin plastic hose which you would wind around one of the top heater hoses which contained hot water and there would be a heat transfer to the washer system - brilliant. Once installed it worked well and was even effective in clearing icing up once the engine was warmed up. There was, so I was to discover one hot summer's day when stuck in a traffic jam, a flaw in the scheme. In a convertible car you are able, at least in the days before cars were more commonly equipped with air conditioning, to feel reasonably smug compared to those sweating inside metal box cars. So sitting in stationary traffic on a hot day somewhere near Westerham in Kent after an earlier quick drive that must have warmed an already hot engine myself and my passenger were rather surprised to be given a hot water shower. The windscreen washers turned themselves on to release the build up of hot water in the system and they wouldn't stop until the water in the system cooled which seemed to take ages. I think we quickly put up the hood so we were hot too and a little damp !

Not long after I had the Spitfire we acquired our first dog. My girlfriend phoned me at work and broached the subject tentatively.

"You know you have said you would like a dog one day - and we both had family dogs when we were children."

I replied in a non-committal fashion with a guarded

-"Yes, why?"

"Well, I have heard of one that is really nice and needs a home. It's not a puppy - it's a lurcher."

At the time this term meant nothing to me - I envisaged a dog with legs of different lengths so that it walked with a gait.

Undeterred, I was told the dog would be brought to see us the following weekend by the owners who had rescued him and already had another large dog and a child and needed Pep, his name, to go to a good home. I envisaged a sort of small terrier and waited seeing our actual potential Pep pet the following weekend with a calm air having been assured we were

under no real obligation! (I was young and naive.)
The following Saturday morning a large estate car drew up in front of the house and the owner took out a large wicker bed before letting a huge long legged dog bound out of the rear door.
They must really pamper their dog - he travels with his own bed - and no wonder they have to re-home little Pep if they have to feed that monster. Anyway, I pondered where is little Pep?
It was only when the owner walked down the path to our front door, carrying the huge wicker bed the size of a large cartwheel that the truth of the situation gradually dawned on me. This huge creature was Pep. There was no small terrier sized lurcher!
Once the door was opened Pep marched in and sat down and eyed us up or rather he looked down on us in a superior fashion as his eyeline was above ours when we were seated. 'So what breed is he actually?' I nervously asked.
"He is an Irish Wolfhound greyhound cross breed and very friendly and intelligent - he loves children.' He looked as if he could eat a couple of small ones for breakfast I thought.
"Does he eat much" I asked.
"He eats anything -he has a good appetite."
The truth of this we found later which I will relate shortly.
He seemed at home and happy. A collar and lead and an improbably large metal feeding bowl with a large bag of dog meal were handed

over and the 'previous' owner left after inviting us to phone if we had any more questions. We were dog owners of one of the largest dogs I had ever seen. Question one - would he fit in the back of the Spitfire - "don't worry my car is a hatchback - he can travel in that" - so I was thinking my treasured two seater would be redundant unless we went everywhere in convoy. I was worrying unnecessarily as Stan, (we never liked Pep and the dog quickly learnt his new name as true to his description was very intelligent,) adapted quickly to life with us and folded himself up in the space behind the seats of the Spitfire. From this position he would put his head between us and closely observe where we were going only pausing to stick his wet nose in one of our ears our to alarm us but

suddenly barking if he saw a dog which with his hound's eyesight he inevitably spotted it before we had, lending a new sense of drama to our journeys. We also found that when travelling with the hood down the wind would sometimes irritate his ears so a sort of tube bobble hat was knitted for him which he happily wore, not minding the hilarity it caused among some spectators in other cars or at the roadside. He had a regal air about him and rightly thought he could carry of this unusual canine sartorial look.

I mentioned earlier that Stan had a healthy appetite and his previous owner said he ate anything. We were to have this confirmed some weeks later when we had arranged a week away in Gower. In preparation we were defrosting the fridge and packing and we went out doing some last minute shopping and filling

the car up with petrol. We had given Stan a long run on the downs that morning where he would tear up and down and swerve at the last minute in front of us.
He had a speed approaching that of his half greyhound ancestry so we weren't surprised that he was fast asleep in his large basket when we went out. On our return it was a different story - he appeared to have gone mad and greeted us at the door with a crazed expression, lips curled and slimy showing large teeth and crouching with his tail between his legs. This was not his normal jolly greeting that the short few weeks of our acquaintance with him had led us to expect. Skirting around him we found his behaviour was apparently one of guilt as the kitchen was a scene of devastation! By a process of elimination we concluded that from the work top and open fridge he had consumed amongst other things two packets of defrosting vegetables, a large tub of butter spread, some eggs and as a crowning glory almost 3 pounds of best Stilton bought the previous weekend in Nottingham market. That afternoon's journey down the M4 required frequent openings of the windows as he subjected the car to his cheesy breath and worse from the other end. By the time we reached Swansea and a friend's flat to stay the night before we collected the keys to our holiday cottage the next day we had all but forgiven him. So we gave him his normal supper and a short walk in the park to 'air him,' before leaving him to sleep, while we went for a quick curry sup-

per, suggesting that it may not be wise for him to join us even if they would let him in. On our return we found his appetite hadn't been completely sated as the large fruit cake baked and brought for our friend had been extracted from our luggage and consumed along with a proportion of the kitchen foil it was wrapped in. Our new companion was certainly some dog! We might have been alerted to this kleptomania had we received at the outset his kennel club certificate which showed his registered name to be Pep Vagabond - very apt, still now to us he was 'Stan the Man.'

The next discovery was a little more alarming as despite his generally affable nature he seemed to take exception to some dogs and would growl and bristle and if challenged by them using his speed and height grab them by their neck and throw them upside down. This was very alarming and embarrassing and the only consolation was that this treatment was reserved for male dogs of a size and strength worth bothering with - Alsatians were a particular target as anything smaller than a Labrador wasn't worth bothering with. It also appeared that the form of conflict was more like a judo bout where once the opponent was upside down on the deck Stan would withdraw wagging his tail leaving the other dog embarrassed and floored. When contacting the previous owners they reluctantly admitted that this had been an 'occasional problem' but they had hoped he had grown out of it. Given that our vet on giving Stan an early once over suggest-

ed he was at least five years old this seemed unlikely.
The most embarrassing incident was when we had gone with a group of friends to a pub unknown to us outside Guidford and had settled down to a round of drinks with Stan asleep under our table after a long walk there.
Unfortunately the pub landlord owned a large German Shepherd dog who casually emerged from behind the bar while the landlord had left to go to the cellar. Stan had not been completely asleep and spotting this potential adversary leapt up overturning our table full of drinks then overturned the shocked resident dog before pursuing him behind the bar where fortunately two of us were able to grab him and drag him back, not without some effort.
The landlord having locked his poor dog away

returned and offered to replace our drinks as 'it was most out of character for his dog to attack another dog who was sleeping!" We drank our drinks and rapidly left before anyone present was able to provide an alternative and more truthful version of events. I don't think we ever went to that pub again - with or without Stan. Returning to the topic of motoring I notice that when looking for some old photos of the car I haven't been able to find a picture of Stan in his hat although I have found one of him in the back of the car wearing a straw hat that I don't think was his. I notice that his occupation of the internal luggage space of the car had forced me to get a boot rack for going away trips and I had forgotten about this. I wasn't to realise this canine acquisition was the first of many compromises that would further influence our choice of cars for some years as we became serial dog owners.

Triumph Stag (or snag)

The enjoyment of open air cars influenced our next choice and it also seemed that I was developing what I believe marketing gurus call a 'brand loyalty.' The enthusiasm for Triumph cars had been helped along by a swap that I had completed with a work colleague who had driven my Spitfire home and loaned me his 2.5 litre Triumph TR6 which was more powerful and at the same time more relaxing with overdrive available on the third and fourth gears, in effect giving a fifth and sixth gears with lower revs. With a fuel injection system and front disc brakes the large engine, almost twice the size of the 1296 cc Spitfire the performance was a revelation. Stated in road tests as producing a respectable 150 bhp, a top speed of 120 mph and accelerating 0 to 60 in just over 8 seconds. I was relieved to return the TR6 safely to its owner the next morning and he commented positively on my car but I had already started to think about a larger engined car.

It is interesting that my earlier Triumph Herald and later Triumph Spitfire were designed by the Italian designer
Giovanni Michelotti and the next car that I looked to acquire was another of his designs - the Triumph Stag.

This turned out to be an unhappy experience. The Triumph Stag was a four seater coupe fitted with a removable hard top and a stow away soft top. It was described as a luxury

tourer and for it's time was well equipped with electric windows, power steering and fuel injection. The quoted performance was impressive for the time and the bulk of the car 0 - 60 time of just over 10 seconds and a top speed of 117 mph from 145 bhp power output. The one we bought was chocolate brown with a tan leather interior and was wonderful, briefly!
We owned the car for less than 24 hours! It was for sale in a small garage on the south coast near where I was working whilst still travelling down daily from Surrey. We part exchanged my girlfriend's car and it was planned that she would take over the Spitfire. Let me just say that motoring enthusiasts now know the model to be something of a problem. Not the design and concept of the car but more the execution of the mechanics and let's be brutally frank here, this was a model from the British Leyland of the 1970's and 80's and worse was to come! The trade in was achieved after work one warm mid summer evening and as we drove through the West Sussex lanes we regretted that the hard top was still attached and we were unable to enjoy open air driving. This minor regret was to escalate as we drove into a country pub car park near home as the healthy V8 engine note was almost drowned out by a high pitched hissing sound and a cloud of steam from under the bonnet. My research into the mechanics of the Stag had revealed doubts about cylinder head problem and overheating but the garage owner had reassured me by producing a certificate claiming

to be a pressure test of the engine as proof the problem would not occur.
The internet carries details of the mechanical shortcomings of the 3 litre V8 Engine used by Triumph including a suggestion that the engine was created by putting together two 4 cylinder Triumph engines that then spent their working life trying to escape from one another. I do know that Triumph Stags were sometimes advertised with replacement 3 litre Ford or Rover engines and stating this as a benefit. Other accusations cited as the cause of the problem was poor siting of the water pump and inherent design flaws in the cooling system; incorrect coolant use and timing chain issues.
Whatever the cause we had to wait a while for the engine to cool down enough to top up the radiator after making our two small 'celebratory drinks' last longer than they would have, particularly if we had been actually celebrating. Then a sedate drive the few miles home with an eagle eyed watch on the car's temperature gauge.
The car was collected by the garage on a trailer the next day and the exchange car returned. We never saw the Stag again and our desire to own one was abandoned although when I have seen one, particularly with the hood down, I do agree they look good.
We never did drive it with the hood down and the experience put paid to my ambitions Triumph wise but we kept the trusty Spitfire for a few more years.

A Stag - but not ours.

A Big Cat

The experience with the Triumph had not put me of getting another car and one day we passed a main Fiat dealer that bizarrely had a beautiful green car on its forecourt at a price similar to that of the ill-fated Stag. After a short test drive we swapped a one year old Fiat for a six year old Jaguar XJ6, complete with a full tank of petrol, or more correctly two full tanks of petrol, a design eccentricity they proved advantageous on a later occasion. The Jaguar was certainly as stylish as the Triumph Stag and proved to be more reliable although it could hardly be less so.

The car was a Mark 1 XJ6 with the less powerful but more economical 2.8 litre six cylinder engine with an automatic gear box. It was marvellous with a walnut dash, wood door cappings and loads of switches and dials and a leather interior much enjoyed by our dog Stan who reclined regally on the back seat able to fully stretch out and without the indignity of his bobble-less bobble hat. He even had his own air outlet for cooling or warming him. One strange thing I noticed the first time I removed the carpets to clean the car were a few sunflower seed shells under them. There were also some strange scratch marks on the top of the drivers seat. I had the fantasy that a previous owner had been a sailor with a parrot but could never prove this despite examining the log book for owners with naval rank titles. The car was automatic with power steering and some

of the controls, I remember for the heating, were air assisted by compressed air to avoid tiring you out using them. They also gave satisfying 'swish' sound as you operated them and the car was so quiet you could hear it!

It was fabulous car and much admired but there were a number of drawbacks. Any spares were expensive - it was a Jaguar so I had a shock when I had to replace a punctured tyre. Secondly I had joined a car club in work to share commuting costs along the Sussex coast to the office in Hove. Whenever there was discussion about which car to

use the group keenly favoured being chauffeured in the Jaguar over their Morris or Peugot. So I seemed to be the designated driver too often. This helped a little with the next drawback - fuel. There was no doubt it was the thirstiest car I had owned to date so any contributions were welcome. There was one party trick in the car which for some design reason was built with two fuel tanks, one in each rear wing with their own locking chrome fuel cap, both holding ten gallons of fuel. On the dashboard in amounts the plethora of switches was one that switched supply from one tank to another when the low fuel indicator light came on. Then magically the needle on the fuel gauge would go up from the red low level to full again. That is if you hadn't already emptied the second tank. This feature was to play to my advantage on one occasioning a garage when having filled one tank the pump switched off and I went into the cashier to explain- and was told, before I could speak, by the already surly elderly garage hitler "that I would have to wait my turn - and young people shouldn't have big flash cars !" So I went back to the pump and waited for the reset. Then filled up the second tank and meekly went in and was only charged for 9 gallons of the 18 I had filled up with. We left rapidly, grinning widely.

The final drawback was more about lifestyle as we were engaged in renovating our home, a flint cottage, and completing much of the work ourselves with visits to reclamation yards and builders merchants as well as avid readers of the local free Ad paper. Using a roof rack we had already collected a garage door, (picked up late at night as the door projected out both sides of the car,) pieces of a conservatory and some long wooden beams and the boot had carried tiles, bricks, bags of cement and plaster as well some ex-butcher shop marble slabs precariously balanced out of a half opened boot. We really needed an estate car and a car that would exceed 20 mpg. So either the Spitfire would go or the Jaguar. Sanity prevailed and the Jaguar was privately advertised and bought by someone to drive it through France to Spain.

The proceeds were enough for some much needed building materials, floor tiles, a new stair and bedroom carpet and the replacement car. I was sorry to see it go.

JPN 65N

Scandinavian Rally Car?

This was bought on the recommendation of a friend and was a new eccentricity: a Saab 95 estate and to a quote a What Car review of the time -"It's eccentric, cramped, costly, old fashioned - and we like it." The only part of that I disagreed with was the 'costly' as we paid £400 - and it was bright yellow. It looked like nothing else at the time and inspired mixed reactions. My work car sharers hated it on sight and it certainly reduced my slots on the rota but we loved it. The car was based on the two door saloon Saab 96 christened the 'woodlice' and similar in shape to the Volkswagen Beetle. It famously won the Monte Carlo rally in the early 1960's and had other rally successes and allegedly was robust enough to be rolled back

upright and carry on driving if it had the misfortune to overturn! Originally the cars had a 2 stroke engine although in our 1974 model this had been replaced by a 1498 cc V4 engine that I was told came from Ford. These origins led to one of its idiosyncrasies. There was a free wheel lever below the dash that was a left over from the two stroke engine. Oil in a 2 stroke arrived mixed with petrol so that when the throttle was closed there would be no lubrication and the engine could seize. To avoid this damage a freewheel device disconnected the engine from the transmission when the throttle was closed. The engine then simply idled but there also would be no engine braking. The effect of this was quite startling. If for example with the freewheel engaged you were driving downhill towards a roundabout, taking your foot of the throttle would lower the revs, the engine would go quiet and you would appear to accelerate silently until you panicked and braked or pushed the accelerator again. Fortunately for drivers of a nervous disposition the freewheel device could be turned off. We used to mainly use it to scare people who hadn't been in the car before. The freewheel would also allow you to change gear without pressing the clutch pedal, again difficult to get used to. The gear change itself was another oddity as it was a column change that also took some getting used to but was ok and quite smooth once you got the hang of it. Driving the car was a complete change from the Jaguar - no power steering or automatic gear change. One luxury the car did have that the Jaguar did not was heated seats but these came on randomly when the car decided it was cold enough and also gave off a burning smell which may just have been dust but in any event we quickly disconnected them. The last thing you wanted when silently coasting down a hill was your seat catching fire!

The car was also an early form of people carrier through having two fold up rearward facing seats in the back. They were only really suitable for two children or one cramped adult but still they were there and a surprise for me whilst looking for the spare wheel. The car didn't have a steering lock but a gearbox lock which locked the car in reverse. I supposed a determined thief could hot wire it and steal it by travelling in reverse - maybe directed by an accomplice sitting in the rear facing seats. Happily no-one was crazy enough to steal it despite, I suspect the unsaid hopes of my lift sharing work colleagues. The car came with a detailed owners manual which along with other useful advice told me how to demist the rear window. It optimistically described how cold air would be blown across the outside of the window by the rear slotted roof spoiler and by setting the front sun visors to be parallel with the roof you could direct warm air blown onto the front windscreen. It sounded highly unlikely but it actually worked. I remembered that SAAB also manufactured jet fighter aircraft so maybe this was their version of the NASA non-stick frying pan spin off. The Saab was great and such a good work horse it persuaded some friends to also acquire one which made for some interesting reactions when out together as one was quite a rarity but you could see people pointing an imagine them saying - "What's that? Blimey, there's another one!"

I do remember one memorable trip back from a night in town with a few drinks when the original plan had been to drive to town and walk home. At the end of the evening one of the ladies in the party was persuaded to drive all six of us home as she had been teetotal all evening. I wisely sat in the pop up kiddy seat in the back while she wrestled with the column gear change whilst trying to see out and ignoring the drunken heckling with dark hints about the scary 'freewheeling option.' She wasn't the friend who was so impressed as to acquire their own example.

Experience with the Saab must have inspired us to explore further the world of Swedish cars because the next acquisition which replaced the Spitfire was a Volvo - but not just any Volvo but said to be the most beautiful model they ever produced and immortalised by no less than Roger Moore in the TV series 'The Saint.'

Saintly Sports

The Volvo P1800 was unlike any Volvo that had been produced up until that time and some car design writers have included it in the listings of

the most beautiful cars ever produced. I realise such listings are very subjective but to look at these lines in the early 1960's it is relatively easy to agree with their enthusiastic response. The long low lines, generous use of chrome, the tail fins and swooping roof line it is easy to see that it was talked about in the same breath as the E type Jaguar. In fact when introduced it was priced similarly to the more powerful and faster E-type. An interesting fact is that the producers of the TV series The Saint starring Roger Moore approached Jaguar to use the new E type as the star's car in the series but the approach was turned down so it was the Volvo 1800 that made its name in the series appearing in 100 episodes and gaining much free publicity. It is said that Jaguar learned from this and keenly offered the later XJS in the late 1970's for the less popular 'The Return of the Saint series.' In truth although it looked incredibly sporty and was by no means slow by the standards of the day it was but it was compromised by having the running mechanicals from the worthy but utilitarian Volvo Amazon saloons and estate cars. The lack of power steering coupled with he weight of the car meant parking could be a bit of a wrestle particularly as visibility of the corners of the car wasn't great.

The car was in pretty good condition for it's age as it was now some 17 years old.Good paintwork and under-sealing for Swedish winters meant that rust the enemy of British cars of the era had been staved off apart from a patch at the bottom of the drivers door. I suspect this had been caused by a worn window seal on the driver's door allowing water into the door lining. Amazingly, a few months after taking ownership the local paper had an ad for a replacement door which I quickly bought. Fitting it was a two person job due to the weight - the doors had heavy side impact doors not common at the time and I narrowly missed amputing one of my feet when the door dropped prematurely after loosening. I don't recall any other work on it other than routine maintenance and for the couple of years I owned it it was as reliable as Volvo's are meant to be. It was much admired and people often incorrectly guessed the maker before seeing the small Volvo badge. Accusations included Ferrari's, Maserati, Alfa Romeo, Lancias and Iso Grifo, some of which were cars in a different price range at the time. The car was a comfortable long distance cruiser and at the time work travel took me across the Southern counties but I would have fancied a run to the Mediterranean or through Northern Europe but other priorities including house renovation

seemed to have got in the way of that. A photo montage of similar cars below may explain the confusion.

Personally, and I am biased, I think the Volvo is the best looking.

Welsh Sports

Before we acquired the Volvo I made a brief abortive attempt to get hold of an even rarer car and not a foreign one, at least not to me. I had heard about a particularly unusual car in the sense that it was not only British but Welsh. The Gilbern Genie and Invader were two door sports saloons produced by Gilbern Cars, a small car company formed in the late 1950's through an unlikely collaboration between Welsh master butcher GILes Smith and BERNard Friese, a German engineer ex -POW who had stayed in the Rhonda Valley after the war. Giles was a butcher living in Church Village near Pontypridd, (the birthplace of another powerful Welsh product - singer Tom Jones.) He discussed buying a fibreglass sports car kit at a chance meeting with a Fries who at the

time was working for a coach builders, Martin who were making fibre glass sports cars. Instead they collaborated and built a on-off Gilbern GT car; amazingly some of the components used were from an Austin A35 my first car.
At the time of my quest I was unaware of this fact. The Gilbern Genie was first produced in 1967 as a 2 + 2 sports Grand Tourer with the new Ford V6 engine either 2.5 or 3 litre and less than 200 are thought to have been produced. The Invader was introduced in 1969 with a tuned 3 litre engine from the Ford Capri 3000 GT, available with manual or auto gearbox and also produced an estate car. Performance was sub 8 seconds 0 to 60 with a top speed of 117 mph. The cars were more upmarket with electric windows, overdrive and

walnut veneered dashboards. The Invader had a production run of over 600 cars between 1969 and 1973.
I have in recent years seen one example - in a museum in Wales but there is an active owners club so I am sure they can still be seen Classic car shows. The early 1980's were the pre internet days and classic car magazines were more limited in circulation than today so I somehow managed to track down someone at the Gilbern owners club and made it known that I was potentially interested in possibly becoming a Gilbern owner. For some days the phone seem to be constantly ringing with current owners anxious to sell their pride and joys. Some even offering to drive halfway across Britain to West Sussex under no obligation for me to buy. I don't know whether it was due to high petrol prices at the time or some inherent problems with the cars but in the event I felt dissuaded to pursue a purchase and I even think we went for long walks with the dog or to the pub to avoid the calls. So I never became a Gilbern owner but still think they look pretty good and also have the unique claim to come from the country of my birth.

More Swede Please

It was a 1977 Volvo 240 saloon in Mustard with brown cloth upholstery and though it wasn't a bad car, in fact it was reliable, powerful, safe and comfortable but ultimately boring. The worst thing was that I had virtually completed a straight swap for the beautiful P1800 coupe - sometimes the sensible option has to be the way. I think I was so unimpressed that I only

seem to have two photos of the car which probably tells a story.
Looking now at the photos it doesn't look like a bad example except maybe the colour scheme and I had completely forgotten it had tow bar but I don't remember towing any thing with it. I remember it was equipped with the Volvo day light running lights and I think the front seats were thermostatically heated for the winter. On reflection we must have been impressed as within twelve months we had traded it in at a local Volvo dealer for a newer 1979 Volvo estate - in a decent colour!

Volvo 245 estate

This was an improvement with power steering, automatic gears, a sliding metal sunroof and a larger engine plus the ability to fit almost anything inside including our 13
stone Irish Wolfhound! For a brief period before we gave the Saab 96 away we were a two Swedish estate car family. On reflection I don't think the Saab was sold, I now recall that we swapped it with a friend for a tent!
The ownership of two estate cars had a benefit one day when S. noticed a council team of workers taking up a section of pavement of red engineering bricks next to the park a couple of roads away. She approached them and asked if they were going to be relaying them. This may not have been the first time that day that they had been asked that question because they had a ready answer about uneven surfaces, cost, danger to wheelchairs etc etc - this was Worthing, after all - the home of the Nimby.
An illustration of this is the Worthing by-pass story. Anyone familiar with the A27 north of the town (once known as an integral part of the aspirational Folkestone to Honiton Trunk road,) will be aware that the dual carriageway west from Brighton abruptly terminates into a normal suburban road for a couple of miles before becoming a modern dual carriageway

again. I am unaware how much of the rest of this trunk dual carriageway has been completed but I am aware it was a matter of some controversy in 1981 when we moved to the town. I was amused to hear a news story earlier this year, some 40 years later, that there was some speculation which of the two pressure groups, pro by-pass and anti , would run out of its elderly members first as they were on average in their late 80's!

My wife did her best to reassure the worker that she was neither a rabid conservationist nor a nimby but politely asked what would now happen to the large piles of perfectly good engineering bricks that were accumulating at the roadside.

"Well Miss, the ones there still here tomorrow we have to load up and take to the council depot and they'll probably be used for hardcore or something."

Sensing an opportunity the question was posed -

'Would there be a problem if a few were taken away to use in our garden?'

"Suppose not -it'll save us moving them but I didn't say that.."

Later that night two Swedish estate cars could be seen from dusk onwards shuttling between the park and our house heavily loaded with enough bricks to construct a very nice brick terrace across the width of the garden at the back of our house.We hope the workmen were pleased to see the depleted piles the next morning but wisely avoided going around to ask them.

I don't remember any problems with the Volvo

estate. I think it passed all MOT's first time and only required the normal routine replacements such as tyres and brakes. It always felt comfortable and safe and was often preferred for long journeys over the more modern company Sierra as a result and not just by the wolfhound. I do remember one journey the length of the M4 to South Wales when Rollo the wolfhound seemed particularly peaceful. It was only when we stopped at the services for a break that we discovered that he had been pre-occupied chewing completely through one of the seatbelts. The experience was so absorbing for him that he chewed through the other one on the return journey despite my having a given him a 'talking to' that he clearly hadn't taken on board. The local Volvo dealer initially refused to believe that a dog could have done this but concluded that he was reluctant to meet our monster dog for corroboration.

As a puppy he had already demonstrated the strength of his jaws and teeth by eating a huge hole in one of the heels of my substantial leather working boots!

The Volvo estate was also a substantial vehicle and it's robustness was something of a liability as I was once warned by a member of her majesty's constabulary when once parking in south London. His exact words as I recall were - "Be sure to always lock your car around here - those are the favourite vehicle for ram raiders as they can back it at speed through a window or wall of a shop, load up and still drive away!" I can believe it - I once reversed into a concrete bollard in a car park knocking it over, denting the rubber bumper -only to find it had reformed it's original shape by the time I arrived home.

Corporate Life

The next chapter in car ownership was to be a dramatic and rather welcome development and a typical 1980's one.
Promotion in work meant I became eligible for one of the holy grails of corporate life - the company car. This was very attractive, no more worries about passing MOT'S or buying new tyres or even more expensive mechanical bills. We were to become a two car family again which was welcome as we were in the process of moving from a town to a much more rural location the dream cottage in the country complete with space around us - a big garden and attached meadow with bridle and footpaths through neighbouring woods. There was even village pub some two miles away through the lanes. Sadly the brand new car wasn't going to be a Jaguar or a Volvo, nothing quite so exotic. At the time my employer was a nationalised industry and there were policies for everything, (some of which to my shame I had authored - still it was a living and apparently somebody had to do it!) The policy was clearly written in an attempt to reduce the unalloyed joy of spending thousands of pounds of someone else's money - in this case the electricity customers in the south east of England - I reckoned most of them could afford it after all it was the most affluent part of the the country.
Rule one - Uk recognised manufacturers only by this they stipulated Ford, Vauxhall and

British Leyland, (no mention of Jaguar, Bentley or Morgan.) and certainly no Ferraris or Maseratis.
Rule 2 - nothing too fancy or exciting so no 2 door coupes, convertibles, or 4 wheel drives. Still it was the first new car I would own and it wasn't going to be my money I was spending. Research was done with car magazines and brochures and as luck would it have it there was a weekend manufacturers car show on the sea front in Sussex. It was decided I would attend along with our fully grown Irish Wolfhound, Rollo some thirteen stones of hair and muscle wrapped up in a still puppyish temperament. We were definitely in the market for another estate car although the ones on offer from the designated approved suppliers were a lot smaller than the Volvo estate he was used to. We looked first at the Vauxhall stand where the offerings were between an Astra or a Cavalier estate. Where or how do car manufacturers dream up their model names. I would have expected the Cavalier to have some frills on the seat or at least an integral hatstand to hang your large floppy hat up on. In truth the choice would have been between the top of the range Astra (which seemed tinny and tiny after the Volvo, or the bottom of the range Cavalier which lacked the hatstands and was a bit dreary.) In the event they took themselves out of the running by refusing to let Rollo try out the rear space for size citing his hairiness. The sales man was rewarded by the dog pushing him in the bum with his wet nose when he had

turned his back on us to securely close the rear door. We moved on to the Ford stand where the Escort estate was immediately dismissed as being too cramped and the only other choice was the Sierra estate. The Sierra was something of a radical change for Ford and initially had been criticised for it's 'jelly mould' shape which was a departure from the more angular designs common throughout the 1970's and 80's. Influential in the concept design was Patrick Le Quément who will reappear later in my story of ownership of extreme cars. Ford helped their cause by allowing Rollo to jump in the back of the estate car on display and the salesman tried to capitalise on this by announcing to onlookers that the estate car could even accommodate a monster dog. Of course Rollo was not over helpful by demonstrating there wasn't really enough room for him to sit up straight so shuffled about sending clouds of dog hair to decorate the interior and causing the car to rock alarmingly from side to side until I felt sorry for both of them and persuaded him to lie down, the dog that is. Which he did with his front legs hanging out the back further belying claims of roominess. I persuaded him to jump out and thanking the salesman moved next door to the British Leyland stand where the salesman was hastily closing all the doors and boot on his Montego estate having observed the antics on the Ford stand next door. Rollo was bored now and dragged me past this over to a food stall where we both enjoyed a hot dog. As some of his was left in his beard I concluded it was probably time to leave

thinking that it looked like we would be ordering a Ford Estate car unless I could persuade the company to supply me with a company Land Rover or Van.
The company car arrived some weeks later a 1.8L estate car in standard white with a sunroof as the only extra.

Quoting from a manufacturer's sales brochure of that year:-
"The Sierra L is a very significant model because it brings Ford's new 1.8 engine into this range. Launched at the same time as the standard setting 1985 models this state of the art power unit features the latest in 'lean burn'

technology for superb economy plus a very strong dash of sporting flavour.
Crisp acceleration and a top speed of 110 mph are one side of the coin. On the other, the 1.8 with its standard five-speed gearbox gives an official 47.1 mpg at 56 mph."
So take that Greta Thumberg - in 1985 manufacturers were becoming hyper sensitive to fuel economy issues!
The brochure goes on to extoll further virtues:-
"Its high technology features also include an electronic ignition system and a twin choke Pierburg carburettor with electric inlet manifold heater controlled by a spark module for cold starts."
All very high tech then and with a space age blobby shape!
My memory of ownership is pretty positive and I don't remember any particular problems with it. I did complain to the company transport department about an intermittent rattle/scratching sound below the dashboard. They offered to look at it when I next needed a service but the problem solved itself when I spotted a mouse in the passenger footwell who was snacking on the crumbs of my mid drive snacks. I was more careful about leaving the doors open when parked near the supplies of duck corn in the garage which was the main attraction for mice in our garden. I only remember two repairs. The first was the replacement of one of the back windows after taking a corner rather enthusiastically and pitching a large metal container carrying a pro-

jector that we had been using in some post SE England 1987 Hurricane presentations as a company PR exercise. This was a minor problem when the car could have been totally written off by the same storm when several huge trees had crashed down in our garden near both our cars. The second was when I borrowed an industrial strength jet washer from the maintenance engineer at the office to give the car a good spring clean after a winter of driving in the muddy Sussex lanes. All was well until I directed the powerful jet of water onto the front spoiler/bumper of the car that must have been plastic and as I played the jet across it the spoiler started to change colour from white to grey as the paint was stripped off. My long suffering corporate transport department arrange a respray for this faulty paint job that I was keen to lay the blame on Ford's poor quality paint. A true white lie.

There was one drawback though. Rollo did fit in the back of the car- just, but for longer journeys his moving about in the back of the car made the car more unstable than felt safe so for weekend trips from Sussex to Wales when he was present we still used the trusty old Volvo estate that seemed heavy and stable enough to cope with his fidgeting. Oh and I remember one other potential problem in that the car had proved to be popular with high sales so that it wasn't always easy to find in a car park in among several others. Also locks being less sophisticated than nowadays I once found that I had unlocked and got into 'my' white estate car to find someone had already broken in and left a briefcase and umbrella on the back seat! Getting out quickly I found my car several spaces away and unlocked it and escaped before potential arrest as a car thief.

Rollo choosing his estate car.

A Bad move

My company car ownership took another turn for the worse three years later when it was time to change the company Ford. For some reason, probably to just have a change, I selected an Austin Montego Countryman in a dreary grey - I don't know what I was thinking- it must have been the luxury of central locking and electric windows. Certainly the ancient Leyland 1600 cc engine can't have been the reason.

It was pretty horrible and I hope being a British Leyland product that it wouldn't last the full three years. My wish nearly came true on one return trip from Wales when rounding a bend we found a car on my side of the road driving toward me! Swerving, hooting, swearing and praying in the split second before impact I could see that the other driver was doing the same thing - to no avail as we collided front offside wing to each other. Both cars had to be taken home on low loaders as they were declared immobile. The accident was just outside the well know Walnut Tree Inn on the Welsh border as we regretfully had been taken a slower more scenic route back to Sussex having decided to have a change from the tedium of the M4 motorway. This proved fortunate as the owners let us use the restaurant phone to arrange RAC recovery and overheard the other driver, an American here on a holiday house swap admitting that he had momentarily

forgot he was in the UK and had used the wrong side of the road.
Some days later I had a call from his insurers withdrawing his admission of guilt and claiming I was driving too fast around the bend and had caused the accident. Somewhat gleefully I was able to point out that we had couple of offices downstairs in our head office where a few cor-

porate lawyers dreamt of contests like this and I would be instructing them to joyously roll up their sleeves and meet him in court. As part of the dispute one of our company solicitors was able to get an independent statement from the restaurant owner stating that he had heard the driver admitting liability. This was all very satisfying but less so was the fact that the Montego was repaired and returned to me for several more months of unexciting motoring. The only other matter of interest relating to this car was the realisation that the model name letter fixed on the back could be rearranged to spell "ME NOT GO." I didn't ever get enough enthusiasm to do this but wish I had.

The Return of the Saab

We kept the Volvo estate car for quite a while and it was trouble free and I am not really sure why we got rid of it as it was replaced by another Swedish workhorse - yes another Saab 95 estate - so good we had to get a second one - in LIME GREEN! I can only think that we found it just too boring to have two sensible cars in the family with the company estate car and the Volvo so it was time for a little more eccentricity. As you have been made aware we had owned one of these Nordic monsters before and this one was pretty much the same apart from a new colour and being a couple of years newer. I guess the designers working in the gloom of the long Swedish winter saw no need to tinker with the earlier design perfection that they had previously achieved. It may be the gloom that persuaded them to produce the car in such vibrant colours like the bright yellow, lime green and there was an orange although a more sober dark brown or blue was available for introverts, (on reflection this was never going to be a car for introverts.) I am pretty sure we paid the same amount to buy it as the first one - the princely sum of £400. We bought it from a second hand dealer working out of a barn and farmyard below the South Downs east Brighton and specialising in 'unusual and sporting cars.' He was advertised as the 'Rocky Horror Car Sales ?' -no idea why as he was quite soberly dressed and the only ec-

centricity; apart from the car we bought, was his question as we paid.
'How many pairs of slippers would you like?" I accepted one pair of moccasin slippers for myself and very comfortable they were. I don't remember much drama with the Saab apart from a complaint from S. that there had been a peculiar smell for a few days and the car needed driving with all the windows open. I suspected the heating elements in the front seats though as it was summer and hot weather they shouldn't have been coming on but I disconnected them just in case. The smell persisted so I checked the exhaust and manifold for leaks and the heater hoses but the smell persisted. I suggested we took out the rubber floor mats, (no deep pile luxury carpet in this no nonsense workhorse.) I found the culprit and called S.
"When did you last buy the dog food?"
She thought it was a fortnight before and at that time the wolfhound was enjoying large quantities of frozen packs of Tripe. One had slid under the front passenger seat where it was fermenting nicely. Two car air fresheners were needed for a few weeks to remove the last traces of the stink.
Swedish cars of that era seemed less susceptible to rust than British and Italian cars of the same age nevertheless the Saab surprised us one day by the tailgate falling in two whilst loading the shopping in supermarket car park. The tailgate had 'hinged' in half and with a boot full of groceries would no longer shut. S.

was helped by a kind stranger who managed to shut the door but only just about avoided being overcome by fumes as the episode occurred before the discovery of the hidden packet of tripe. Whether he thought a new eau de cologne was being road tested he didn't say but once the door was fixed he beat a hasty retreat - probably gasping for fresh air.
It seemed that a fractured rear window seal on the tailgate had allowed a serious amount of hidden rusting to develop.
In those days before Ebay and the internet the main source to find spares was the weekly "Exchange and Mart" publication and luckily the Swedish Car Parts centre was able to supply one - and in the same colour. Some days later the postman delivered the biggest and certain-

ly the heaviest parcel I had received up to that time. I remember fitting it was not the easiest job and needed more than four hands. Luckily the errant tripe pack had by now been located and removed so at least breathing was an option.

Another Saab!

We must have been pretty enthusiastic about Saabs as the lime green estate was replaced by another one, this time it was a 96 saloon. It was advertised locally and described as restored and had been resprayed a bright canary yellow.
I think we must have put in the Saab estate as part exchange and I remember that it was rusting and may have failed the MOT. Although the restored yellow saloon looked like an improvement on the green rusting estate experience proved, as with a number of our purchases, that it wasn't necessarily a wise buy. I think all was well initially and the older car, it was 1971 reg to the estates 1975, attracted some comments on the good condition.
We began to suspect that the restoration was perhaps a cosmetic one. The two previous Saabs had been pretty reliable, starting ok and generally mechanically sound. The new one started to exhibit some temperamental behaviour - refusing to start, suddenly stalling and generally unreliable electrics. The car had been bought from a small time car dealer who operated out of a farm in a nearby village and it started to be a regular occurrence to call him out because the car had come with some rudimentary six months warranty. For some reason the dealer became to be known to us as cowboy Dave - I believe he wore a wide rimmed hat but in those days 'a cowboy' was a derogatory term used for shady or unreliable

tradesmen. The term is probably outlawed now as racist to cowboys and indeed the term 'out-

lawed' may also be prohibited - it's hard to keep up with current dictates. In any event

Cowboy Dave proved more reliable than the car in coming to rescue S. even providing a replacement vehicle form his stable of unreliable and bizarre cars. It may be that all his cars were bizarre or alternatively as we had bought the Saab from him he might have thought we preferred eccentric vehicles. The favourite loan was a square, tinny Fiat Panda 4 x 4 in fluorescent orange with an engine that sounded like a lawnmower. I don't remember what other strange substitutes we were entrusted with and it wasn't usually me that was driving them and being rescued. There's not much else to say about the yellow Saab other than the adage appearances can be deceptive was certainly true and the two less glamorous estate cars were better purchases. I think we must have sold the car back to Dave, no doubt at a loss- still he did deliver substitute cars to wherever it broke down which isn't a bad service for a car that must have cost less than a thousand pounds.

An Italian Job

I wish I could say the replacement was a more sensible purchase but I can only think the orange Panda 4 x 4 had whet our appetites for driving Italian exotica. This was the 1990's and the cool car to have was a VW Golf GTI especially a convertible (or cabriolet) as they were more exotically named. As a second car our budget didn't stretch to topless Teutonic reliability but another small local garage had an Italian doppelgänger on it's forecourt. A four seater convertible Fiat Strada ! Yes, as advertised at the time 'a car build by Robots!' -(and possibly bought and driven by dummies!) As I think the photo shows it wasn't a bad looking car and we were obviously taken in by it as from memory I think it cost £900. In the garage it was on display with the hood down and it must have been the summer, so that was how we test drove it, but just as we were taking ownership the garage guy muttered something about the hood needing adjustment to fit properly but undaunted and sold on the idea of open air motoring again for the first time since the Spitfire we drove away in it with the wind whistling through our hair. Although the hood did go up the fit did not look weathertight so a scan of the car spares classifieds found that a similar hood complete with frame could be found in a scrap yard near Aldeburgh, not exactly round the corner but probably the only one available outside Italy. There was plenty of room for the whole hood assembly in

A284 EGY

A284 EGY

the company car, the Renault Espace so £30 later after a walk on the east coast beach we were on our way home.
My research has reminded me that the model was designed for Fiat by the famous Bertone design house who were the creators of much more expensive and exotic models for the marques of Lamborgini, Maserati, Alfa Romeo as well as others. The designs included the 1950's Alfa Romeo BAT cars thought by many to be the most beautiful cars ever designed.

The Fiat shared many things with these beautiful cars but unfortunately these seemed limited to - they had four wheels, one in each corner, a steering wheel inside, some seats, a petrol engine and they were constructed out if metal.... and that's about it. In the case of the Fiat it felt that the metal had been economised a little too much and the doors shut with a cheap clang rather than an expensively reassuring clunk. The car was also rather over designed in the dashboard area with more confusing instrumentation and buttons than the car seemed to require. A brochure photo below I think conveys this. I seem to recall some rudimentary economy gauge that suggested your driving style that definitely didn't seem vey Italian.The car always felt a bit flimsy and the engine a bit enthusiastic for the construction of

the bodywork. Eventually the need for a more

reliable second car happily coincided with a more prosperous financial position and it was time for an upgrade. A sensible saloon car or an economical hatchback - of course not !

Turning Japanese

Yes the new car was to be our first from the land of the cherry blossom and as the photo shows we were trying our hardest to make it feel at home with us. A friend had recently been enthusing about his own Suzuki, its build quality, reliability and the benefit of 4 wheel

drive in winter weather. We were living in pretty rural area and the High Weald was given to snow falls much heavier than down on the Sussex coast. A trip to a Suzuki dealers allowed us to try out a couple of Suzuki models and we soon concluded that the 4 door Vitara was bigger than we needed. The Samarai, despite the aggressive macho name was a bit too small but we concluded that the 2 door Vitara would better suit our needs but at the time the dealer could not obtain one for several months. A scan of the classified ads locally discovered a nearly new one for sale nearby. The sellers seems genuine with an expectant mother needing a different car and after a test drive the sale was agreed. The car was metallic black with both hard and soft tops with the hard top taken home in pieces in the Espace. The hard top had the advantage of a glass rear window with a heating element so it was agreed that we would fit that later in the year for the winter. The Suzuki was a 1.6 litre JLX SE with 95 bhp and a 5 speed gearbox switchable to four wheel drive and equipped with power steering, electric windows and central locking.

Mentioning the equipment, much of it electrification of previously manual operations, e.g. electric elements in windows or mirrors for demisting . Previously this would be achieved by wiping the condensation of windows with a duster which would then be stuffed away in a glovebox (were they ever used for storing gloves?) to hopefully dry out or possibly to encourage a coat of mildew on an adjacent surface. My current car not only supplies satellite navigation through a screen but supplements it with traffic and speed camera warning, weather and news flashes and if required web searching through a wi-fi browser app. Almost unlimited music can be played from Apple music player and the album cover and song listing displayed in colour on the screen. Such developments if viewed in my first car would have seemed the stuff of science fiction.

The Vitara certainly felt more solid than the Fiat and proved very reliable throughout our ownership. In fact although we lost track of it after trading it in in 2004 an enquiry on a Carcheck site reveals that it went on for another dozen years with its last MOT pass recorded in March 2016.
Using the website carcheck.co.uk has proved to be a mildly distressing experience as I have found very few of my old cars to be legally on the road. The biggest shock was that the bizarre 2003 Renault (more later) still has a current MOT. 2003 must have been a good year but its less surprising that my little Honda manufactured the same year is still going strong. My 1979 Spitfire was legally on the road until 2014 some thirty years after our ownership. Others have been less successful with none of the company cars surviving. We enjoyed ownership of it so much that we hired Suzukis on several occasions on holidays in Crete only defecting to Korean smaller cars once we realised the benefits of air con in the mediterranean sun. The Land Rover pictured was not ours and was likely to be a company loan car whilst the Alfa was 'resting' or throwing a temper tantrum but it serves to show the smaller Vitara could not be accused of being a bullying Chelsea tractor.

R354 WOF
VITARA
K27 KWV

Spaceship

The next breakthrough in car ownership came about as a result of the government's privatisation programme where my regional electricity company was floated as a plc, i.e. a public limited company. Along with personal contracts, new job titles and share options, the previously restricted list of approved manufacturers was expanded to include other European car makers. This was eagerly embraced by managers in the company and soon our car

park was filling up with gleaming new BMW's and bottom of the range Mercedes. Neither of these appealed to me but at last a company van was a possibly or more correctly an MPV in the form of a Renault Espace. This was the mark 2 Espace and to my mind an improvement over the boxy first attempt.

Certainly the load carrying ability was very attractive apart from anything else but this car was to provide new levels of auto equipment to my car ownership. Central locking with an alarm, aircon - essential with all the glass, a decent stereo with multi cd player and controls on a stalk for the driver, 7 seats in a number of permutations it was even possible to swivel the two front seats around to face the two at the very back with a single seat folded down in the middle to form a table. The new car 'must have' for some reason was cupholders and it had lots of these.

The Espace was my first car equipped with air conditioning, common in cars nowadays but much rarer then and the Espace had a particularly powerful unit. I would delight in putting it down to the coldest setting and putting the fan on full it was possible to see peoples breathe condensing and getting them shivering when I would innocently enquire whether it was cool enough yet.

The load carrying was tested early on when I discovered that the data centre at work had loads of clean wooden pallets to dispose of and by removing all the five rear seats I could bring home seven or eight of these to construct giant compost ins in the garden - most useful.

The car had a 2 litre injection engine with ABS brakes and despite its size was relatively light so gave a relatively spirited performance for such big vehicle of that era. Some of this was down to the so called space age composite body panels - probably some kind of plastic, I guess.

It would be good to be able to say that all this sophisticated European design meant the car was reliable and a joy to own and drive and it was - apart from one memorably scary incident when the car appeared to be taken over by evil spirits!

Returning to Sussex along the eastbound M4 one evening after a work trip I was rather shocked to see all the warning lights on the dashboard starting to flash on and off randomly. I quickly pulled over onto the hard shoulder and turned off the ignition. I was just about to restart it and hoped the warning lights would go out when the engine started itself. I took the key out of the ignition and got out grabbing my coat and briefcase. Standing beside it, holding the ignition key I was mystified that the engine was still running. Then I had a brainwave and using the remote control ignition key locked the car calculating that the immobiliser would cut the ignition which it did but for some reason the alarm then went off. Pressing the key to unlock it only took a few seconds before the engine started itself again and I am standing outside holding the ignition key. I know that today using remote apps it is now possible to start your engine remotely and even drive a car remotely into a parking space but this technology wasn't to my knowledge available in the mid 1990's unless I had unbeknown to me been provided with some advance future car technology test-bed car by Renault. So it was a choice - car locked, engine off but alarm going - or alarm off and the engine running.

Luckily my company mobile phone had been upgraded from an in-car model to one that could be removed and worked outside so I rang the RAC which we had membership through the company. They took the details of the last junction I had remembered passing and told me to wait away from the car and asked if I had noticed any burning smells or smoke. There might have been some rubber on the road either from stopping or me sprinting from the car but I avoided mentioning this. They warned me the response time could be over an hour and that the fire brigade might attend as it sounded electrical - I was tempted to suggest calling Ghostbusters but remembered they were fictional. So I sat up on the grass bank and phoned home and explained that I was likely to be delayed and 'Yes - the car alarm was ours but if I switched it off I was fearful of the car driving away by itself.' I was tempted to open the car again and switch on all the electrics to try and run down the car battery as quickly as possible and shut off the the alarm but in truth having explained the bizarre symptoms three times including twice to the RAC who I am not sure believed me at the first telling I was now a little scared of the car and wary of going to near it. It was quite a pleasant spring evening and could have been quite peaceful sitting above the quiet motorway were it not for the insistent car alarm. This was soon drowned out, unfortunately by a fire engine siren which was coming from a full sized fire engine as it roared up and stopped behind the 'possessed car' and disgorged several firemen - two in suits with breathing apparatus and the one without asked for the keys and tried to understand what I was saying over the double noise of both the alarm and the siren which they hadn't switched off yet. Once the car was unlocked they went to open the bonnet but of course the engine started which certainly startled the fireman who was about to stick his arm into the engine despite me explaining about the problem. So we went through the locking the car to stop the engine routine and then shouted at each other over the alarm which thankfully was no longer accompanied by their siren. This was now silent maybe because having now had enough excitement from having a limb potentially removed they had decided to calm things down a bit. One fireman disconnected the battery and while he came over to tell me this his colleague who would appear to be still enjoying his own adrenalin rush filled the engine compartment with a fire extinguisher, (a large one!) of foam. I was past caring so wishing them a thanks and goodbye. I waited for the RAC recovery vehicle hoping it would be before dark as I couldn't put the car's lights on. Remembering there was a breakdown triangle in the boot I cautiously walked fifty yards back down the hard shoulder and put that up as a precaution. Thankfully, the RAC man arrived before sunset and a couple of hours later I was dropped off home with the car being collected by an apologetic mechanic from the Renault dealer for another low loader trip and I was left with a replacement car which hopefully was less autonomous. Some days later the sales manager rang up full of apologies and the usual excuse of this has never happened before to his knowledge allowing me to say that was of little comfort to me as it had happened in every Renault Espace I had ever owned and I was not impressed.Upon the return of the errant car it was explained to me that the wiring loom had

been completely replaced as it was too tight passing into the engine bay from the behind the dashboard and there was a suspicion a rubber insulating grommet was missing. this has frayed and shorted and luckily had not caused a fire. it was a little while before I trusted the car enough to be good friends again.

Ford Again

When it was time to replace the Renault - the company allowed this every three years it was always an opportunity to try something else and at somebody else's expense the risk seemed minimised. We had got used to the space, flexibility and higher driving position of the Espace so I looked around for an alternative in the range that had come to be called 'people carriers.' A ridiculously redundant term as surely this was a feature of all cars and other vehicles. Nevertheless the market for these was growing in popularity and Ford had joined the market with a joint development with VW - the Ford Galaxy and the VW Sharan. Now call me old fashioned but I didn't fancy owning a Sharon or even a Sharan, no offence -it's a lovely name but at least the Galaxy shares it's title with something astronomical - and a chocolate bar! In any event the Ford was better value in my allowed price range, probably because the company bought a lot more Ford vehicles, mostly Transit vans, than VW's -I don't know or maybe it was a badge premium exercised by the German company as the models were virtually identical. The car was to be a Galaxy 2 litre Ghia and petrol of course as it was the early days of the ill judged 'let's all move to more economical and greener (!) diesel engines.' What a cul-de-sac that has turned out to be that we drove up.
As cars were becoming to more alike in appearance and some of this was down to aero-

dynamics and drag coefficients it was not always easy to select them based on brand. In fact a friend who was also entitled to a company car claimed to select his on two important criteria - how comfortable the drivers seat was, (he drove all over the country and parts of mainland Europe') and how easy it was to operate the sound system and how loud it was! I am sure this simplified things when he was not seduced by issues if branding and design.
I am not so single minded and swayed by the upmarket luxury features of the Ford Ghia model, (that's what the brochure said) I se-

lected a metallic maroon model that's lets be realistic here is basically a van with more windows and stuffed full of thick carpet

and six armchairs in a hideous grey patterned velour that could have come from the DFS nouveau bilious range.
It was well equipped with the so called 'luxuries' including an electric sunroof, six electric windows, cd multi player, heated front windscreen, climate control, rear heater controls and enough map reading and courtesy lights to equip a xmas tree amongst other refinements.It was even possible to order a 12 volt small fridge that clipped in place instead of one of the rear seats so we had one of those as an extra and very civilised it was too for picnics.
Mechanically it was a 2.0 litre DOHC Ford petrol engine with ABS and traction control and described by ford's marketing department as 'providing lively performance with impressive economy.' The power output was an increase over the Renault, (115 BHP as against 105,) the Ford was considerably heavier at a kerb weight (what is that?) of 1650 Kg to the lighter Renault's 1320 Kg. The 'lively performance' of 12 seconds 0 to 60 and 110 top speed doesn't sound so impressive by modern standards to-

day but despite its weight it was livelier than the Espace (claimed 0-60 of 13.5 seconds.) The extra weight did make it feel more solid and stable but maybe the armrests on the seats helped with that.
In fact I always felt the Renault could use more power and some lunatic at Renault agreed but maybe went a little too far. To celebrate the tenth anniversary of Renault's Formula 1 involvement the Espace F1 show car was developed. Using a carbon fibre reinforced body and chassis a 3.5 litre V10 engine from a 1993 Williams-Renault FW15C car mounted mid engine in the car and powering the rear wheels via a race car semi-auto gearbox.
The performance was electrifying:- 0-60 mph in 2.8 seconds and 0-124 mph in under 7 seconds plus a top speed of 195 mph!
I wouldn't mind a go in that although there was no room behind the front seats for passengers and it apparently got a little too warm inside for an Irish Wolfhound.

I am racking my brains to think of any memorable experiences of a galactic or otherwise nature whilst owning the car. Maybe its the way with Fords - as with the Sierra, it just does what it says on the tin!

Italian again!

It all very well having 'people carriers' for collecting things and being the nominated driver on outings after work to the pub -"well you've got an hour's drive home anyway and your car can take all six or seven of us!" Also the novelty of driving around in a glass box sitting in an armchair pales after a while particularly when at the time of ordering the company car for the next three years there is a new Alfa Romeo saloon announced said to be their best car for some time. It was time to drive a proper car again.

The car was a four door saloon but the design made it look more like a two door coupe with the rear door handles incorporated and disguised in the window surround. A nice touch but confusing for passengers. I had ordered the top of the range 2.5 v6 24 valve with a six speed manual gearbox in a beautiful powder blue with a light tan leather interior and tasteful alloy wheels and if I say so myself it looked stunning. The engine had a powerful Alfa style throaty exhaust which on my first trip into the company car park caught the attention of my boss, the Chief Exec as he was getting out of his rather anonymous large dark Mercedes bracing himself for a full day of corporate squabbling. He called across to me in an unusually tetchy manner as we were normally on good terms with one another. I sensed he had got out of bed maybe the wrong side that morning or was anticipating a particular difficult day at the top.

"Is that a company car? Is it within the policy guidelines?"

'I am sure it must be - I think it was cheaper than it looks,' I said in what I hope was a reassuring tone.

"Doesn't look blooming cheap !" he replied before walking quickly into the office.

I avoided getting in the lift and instead took the stairs hoping to avoid further awkward questions and planning to ring the Transport manager suspecting the CEO might be planning to call him. I was also wondering whether my purchase of the fridge for the last company car had not gone unnoticed and was 'coming home to roost,' so as to speak.

The line for the transport manager was engaged and fending off questions from colleagues who had noticed not only my sparkling

new car but the exchange of words in the car park - I set the call to ring back. When it did I started to explain that Richard might get a call from the CEO about my car and the transport entitlement policy but before I could finish he said John's already been on - he was refusing to believe that your outrageous looking car was within the policy but I think I reassured him. Thanking him it seemed the matter was closed but I thought it safer to park around the corner away from the CEO's reserved space for a week or two. I think the plush leather interior and luxurious wooden dash inserts might have sent him over the edge.

One of the unique things about the Alfa was that it was worth opening the bonnet. This is a relatively unusual experience with modern cars in contrast to my earlier memories of my Dad's

Ford Anglia that seemed to require at least one 'head under the bonnet ' moment on any outing further than a few miles. With modern cars and particularly company ones the normal practice is to open the bonnet when the windscreen washers run out or at least look like they are about to. No with the Alfa, at least initially, there were two reasons - the first one was to admire the engine block itself. Unlike most other modern car engines that I have seen that resemble a central heating boiler with black plastic shrouds and covers the Alfa engine was a thing of real beauty as this photo from the sales brochure shows.

The alloy of the cylinder heads were branded with the Alfa Romeo logo in raised crimson lettering whilst this was complemented by chrome pipes that must have helped to make the musical engine notes.
The second reason for the regular opening of the bonnet was given by the sales lady at the handover. This particular model had some fancy engine oil recommended for it and I was warned that it was recommended to check the oil level weekly! This seemed a bit of an overkill in a modern car but I carefully obeyed this regime and sure enough it did consume oil and the recommended oil must have been a mixture of myrrh and sturgeons liver oil judging by the price for a can which admittedly came with the Alfa crest on it. Subsequent purchases made their way through my monthly expense account. Still at least the engine was a thing of beauty to admire whilst regularly topping up.

Unfortunately opening the bonnet was something that had to be done on a few occasions during ownership but not always by me. Whether it was the enthusiastic way it encouraged you to drive or an inherent fault in the model's elections and engine management it was after all an early release so much so that strangers came up to you frequently to enquire what the car was. Nevertheless it did on several occasions put itself into safe mode restricting the revs and showing an engine warning light on the dash needing a call to the dealer

and company transport manager who always took this news with some glee. He was of the opinion that the Alfa was not a suitable company car, maybe remembering the earlier conversation with the CEO about the car. The transport people also took delight in supplying me with unlikely replacement cars. This may have been after the Alfa dealer briefly supplied me with a bright red two seater GTV was a warranty replacement and although it looked gorgeous I felt driving it was like looking through a letter box and a little disconcerting seeing the world hurtling towards you in it. Once the transport department were involved they tried two approaches. Firstly, to avoid me giving them more grief it felt they were plotting for me to kill myself by providing unfamiliar 'hairy' cars such as an Audi Quattro which tempted speeding by feeling glued to the road. Another time they supplied some boring looking Ford Granada saloon that turned out to have a cosworth engine and was both rapid and horrible. A different approach was in the form of a 'non turbo' diesel Land Rover Discovery in which you would ambitiously pull out into traffic gaps only to find the snail like acceleration felt you were in the process of parking. They also dumped some large Rovers on me which I usually felt too embarrassed to drive anywhere not owning a pipe and slippers.. All was well once the 156 was returned - at least until the next time.
Amazingly I didn't collect any speeding tickets in the Alfa although S. did once. It was not dif-

ficult as the car urged you to drive it. Once when away on holiday it suited me to leave it in the company car park which was near to Gatwick and I left the keys with a colleague and friend at work. On my return I asked Arthur if he enjoyed the loan but despite having owned an Alfa Spider previously he quietly admitted that he had found the 156 'too involving' for the morning commute to the office so had limited it to a couple of drives. Maybe he just thought a fortnight's commute would test the Alfa's reliability.

Multiplication

They say work expands to fill up the time you are there - Parkinson's Law? Living in the country with a lot of space and a large gravel parking area this concept may also apply to parking spaces and cars. The family fleet consisting of a series of company cars of varying interest as well as more interesting but cheaper, normally older and less reliable second family cars. But the driveway looked a bit too spacious. It was time to enter the dangerous world of the Classic Car. Let me warn you this is one slippery slope.

You start of by rationalising that these older 'Classic' cars are simpler and easier to self-maintain. You will only be doing low milage so insurance will be cheap and there may not be road tax to pay. Because it won't be an every day car it can be more exotic, convertible? impractical? even unreliable but with character. You won't need complicated modern equipment as they will be driven on the last friday in the month and on sunny weekends possibly to car rallies and events in fields with car owner clubs and members in tweed caps and tank tops. And these things are meant to attract you ? or is it the nostalgia effect and the ability to own something rarer and needing care and attention.

Our own entry into this rarified world was by means of a 1966 Volkwagen split screen camper van at a time when they could be bought at a modest price without needing a mortgage sized sum, I understand good examples now fetch tens of thousands! I had always liked the look of these small van type vehicles and after going to a car rally event in Bexhill in Sussex and seeing a few examples with camping interiors I started looking through classified adverts to find one. The appeal of having a van type vehicle again for collecting furniture and garden supples etc coupled with the idea of a camping in (relative) comfort was a strong motive. Though in the first weeks of ownership I was mildly horrified to learn that my wife had arranged for me to collect several very large bags of horse manure for the garden from the local stables - "It's free and I am sure the smell will have gone by the time we go camping - anyway you haven't put a camping interior in yet so this is a good opportunity while there's room in it!" - unarguable!

She was right - the vehicle I found was to the north of us in Kent, outside Sevenoaks and was described as an unfinished project. When we viewed it the owner seemed very genuine and explained he had already a newer and bigger camper van as his physio had diagnosed hi back trouble down to the driving position in the VW. He was well over six feet tall and when I saw how he was hunched over the wheel on the demonstration run I had no difficulty coming to the same conclusion. The test run was one of the more thorough ones I had experienced as we dashed around the country lanes serenaded by the engine noise under the floor

in the back and he demonstrated it's ability to hill climb due to something called 'reduction boxes?' I was impressed and it came with a full MOT and was tax exempt so the following weekend we collected it for a thrilling drive home. The steering was fine, gear change ok, once mastered but the all round drum brakes needed you to deploy a certain amount of anticipation of events ahead. This was helped by reasonable visibility from the raised position and also from a heightened nervousness from your proximity to the front of the vehicle and the abundance of metal rather than soft plastic dash or airbags in front of you. Still it was safely navigated home and it was time to take stock of what we had.
For those unfamiliar with the Split screen or 'Bulli' as it is known in its native Germany it has a rich history and amazing versatility.

The type 2 VW, (the earlier VW Beetle saloon was the Type 1) could possibly lay claim to be both one of the most versatile and longest living vehicles to date. The first type 2 the split screen began production in 1950 and carried on until 1967 with production in South America going on for several more years. All told it is estimated that 1.8 million models of the 'Splitty' were produced and for its age a large number are still on the road today. Its origins are unusual and unlikely with an international flavour. At the end of the second world war in 1945 the huge Volkswagen factory at Wolsfburg was placed under the control of the British REME, (Royal Electrical and Mechanical Engineers) and a major Ivan Hirst was in charge of production of VW beetle cars. As production stepped up it was apparent that transport was needed for components within the sprawling factory particularly after some loaned British

Army fork lifts had to be returned. Some development engineers drafted some ideas for a vehicle using a VW chassis and a drivers seat at the back and a number if these were made and used in the factory.

A Dutch Volkswagen importer, a Ben Pon saw the vehicles and came up with the idea of creating a box like all purpose load carrier based on this design but moving the driver to the front and his rough sketch is shown below.

Pon's idea was developed through 1948 with

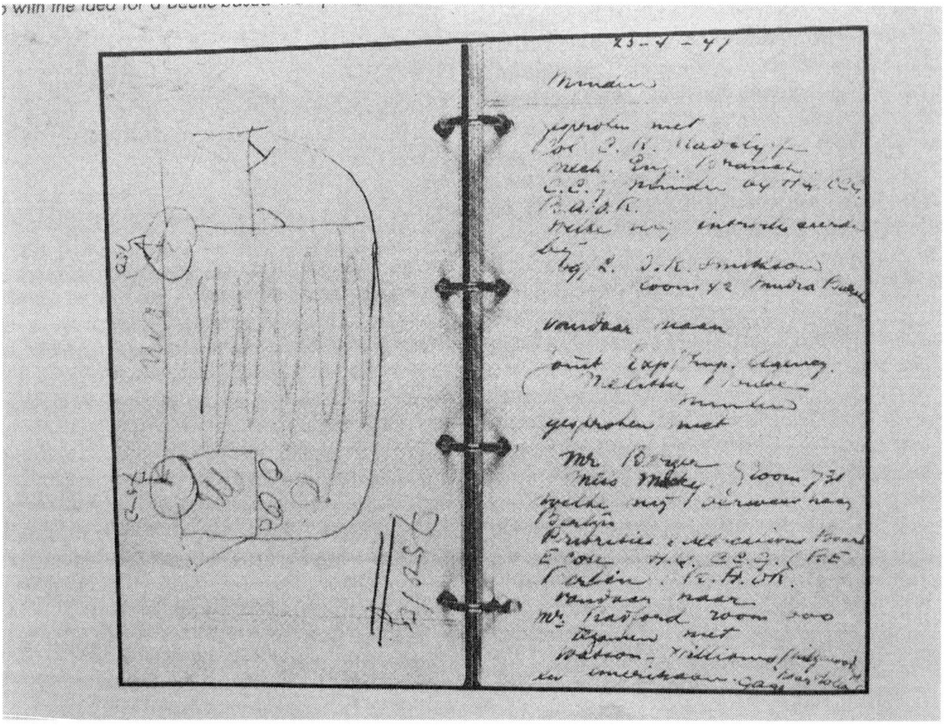

prototypes being produced and refined through 1949, strongly supported by the new German CEO at Wolfsburg, Heinz Nordhoff. In May 1949 six demonstration vehicles were produced, 4 were closed panel vans but 2 were specialised one of which was a minibus with seating for eight or nine. So even at it's inception the versatility of the vehicle was recognised. It was designed to carry a load equivalent to its own weight with the load space accessed by double doors in the centre of the vehicle, between the engine and fuel tank in the rear and the driver and passenger in the front. This made for optimum balance and stability when loaded and with a load capacity of 162 cubic feet at almost two thirds of the total volume of the vehicle it was a box on wheels. The central double doors made it efficient for loading whether it was for goods, people or camping gear. This is one of the 1949 prototypes, so close in design to my 1966 model.

The flexibility of the pure design is clearly reflected in the wide range of uses the vehicle has been adapted and used for. The basic box shape has been used for a standard van, minibus, fire engine, ambulance as well as a range of camper vans by a multitude of conversion companies as well as amateur conversions such as ours.

Adaptions of the original model on the same floor pan has produced a single and double cab pick up as well as a high roofed van.

GEMEINDE
TITISEE
NEU-M 234

Our own example was blue and white with a vinyl sunroof and a bench seat in the front with the back behind a metal bulkhead that hid the spare wheel currently empty and all carpeted in grey loop carpet -including the door backs and the lower side panels.
I think this gave a certain amount of sound insulation although the engine noise was more intrusive than any car I had previously owned - not unpleasant - a friendly burbly sound that just got louder and changed pitch under pressure. I say the rear was empty and it was apart from a 'rock and roll' bench bed frame that hadn't been fitted but would double as a rear bench seat and convert into a bed. Under it I discovered another vent into the car that I think should allow warm air from the heat exchangers (more later) but currently brought in more engine noise until i temporarily blocked it with a large sponge. The passenger compartment was accessed by twin doors almost like railway carriage doors and at the back over the engine compartment there was a large hatchback tailgate. There was a small door below giving access (not great access) to the engine - a 1600 cc air cooled engine as used in some of the more powerful VW Beetle cars.
Once acquired we started to fully embrace the VW ownership experience - it was like joining a cult albeit a friendly and positive one. There

were clubs, magazines, books, web sites as it was the earlier days of internet use, as well as meets and auto jumbles to attend . A new world opened up to us but first of all I needed to make the Bus as it was known equipped for camping. All the resources of magazines etc were going to help with this but it was also a great excuse to go to auto jumbles and root around among pile of old bits and pieces and this provided the basics to equip the Bus as a camper. We had also enrolled in the SSVC -the Split Screen Volkswagen Club with their monthly magazine and website and before long we had become members of the SVOC - not a breakaway group due to some historic falling out but the local Sussex Volkswagen Owners Club - it was taking us over. Through one of these links I managed to source a kitchen unit, an ingenious plywood and stainless steel unit housing a small cooker with grill, cool box in a cupboard , and the proverbial kitchen sink and draining board! I think it cost me £30. This had the makings of a project as fitting it required a 12 volt pump for the tap, drilling a hole for the drainage and fitting a gas cylinder and regulator for the stove. Yes, we were cooking on gas now! Seating and sleeping was the next project and more drilling holes in the poor old bus followed and being scared of rust in old cars i was careful to repaint the bare metal where it was drilled as a precaution. This was followed by an original VW camper roof cupboard, above the engine compartment, and found at an auto

jumble. Below this I constructed two wooden side cupboards as a larder and storage.
The converted bed when folded down was just 3 foot 6 wide -hardly a double bed but comfortable if no-one moved around too much and the dog had to be discouraged from joining us on it. We now owned a rescued collie/ golden retriever cross -smaller than the wolf hound -what isn't, but a dog with real character. He enjoyed travelling on the front bench seat between us, paying a lot of attention almost as if he was learning to drive, cocking his head to one side if I changed gear or turned on the wipers or indicators. He was also delighted that we were travelling in a vehicle containing food

in the larder cupboard or fridge as well as his bed blanket - he was a natural and enthusiastic camper.

The classic Volkswagen fraternity is I believe the most active and largest in population of any car marque. I am aware that MG owners, Mini's and Jaguars among others have active clubs , rallies and shows but the VW scene is large scale. Most weekends, (at least outside the winter months, for heating is not a strong point for air-cooled cars) there is some kind of large scale meet somewhere in the country. We attended many of them on sunny summer days, wet spring weekends and chilly autumn evenings. The annual London to Brighton run is a particular highlight of the calendar and I believe we attended five on the trot.

In this several thousand classic VW cars and Vans with their owners and passengers assemble in south London many camping overnight then bleary eyed and possibly and having consumed a fried breakfast their vehicles are driven in a cloud of exhaust smoke and a not inconsiderable slick of oil towards to south coast to assemble along the seafront in Brighton. Like the wartime Atlantic supply conveys not all of them make it and it's quite sad to pass vehicles undergoing running repairs at the roadside as you pray you won't be the next to succumb. The VW fraternity is very friendly and not very judgemental about your age, occupation or your vehicle. So often you are exchanging comments and hints about your vehicle with guys a generation younger. This bonhomie can have its drawbacks as we found out during an overnight stay at a show in Oxfordshire when during our conversation with a couple about their camper van awning our dog helped himself to half of their fried breakfast out of their pan cooking on the ground over a camping stove. They took it in good part although I am unsure if they ate the rest. As I said earlier camping was very popular with our collie cross.

On another outing we had a heated drama of our own. We had been on a 'cruise' in convoy along the Sussex coast with some dozen other VWs from the Sussex club. Fortunately there were a couple of VWs behind us at the time when I was aware of the engine starting to misfire so looking in the rear view mirror to see if I could safely pull over I was rather horrified to see clouds of smoke in our wake and Danny in the car behind flashing his headlights and waving that we should pull over which I did, quickly. We both jumped out of the bus taking the trusty dog with us and could smell a strong burning odour from the rear of the car. When I opened the rear engine lid the inflow of air caused a small fireball to erupt from inside the engine and at that moment Danny who was in the car behind had the foresight to have his classic car owners friend to hand - the fire extinguisher! The flames went out only to reappear but thankfully less fiercely and I was able to put them out with our own fire extinguisher. We were pretty shaken up having read of tales in the Volkswagen press of camper vans being completely burnt out by engine fires and also aware that the metal fuel tank was also in the engine bay -plus the calor gas bottle inside the bus - along with plenty of other flammables such as bed cushions, carpets and curtains. It seemed we had a lucky escape and I was indebted to Danny's quick fireman's act. Being an optimist I wondered if it would still start so with Danny watching the engine from a few yards away I tentatively got back in and turned over the starter. I heard him shout Stop! Stop! which I did and got back out and joined him looking into the engine bay. The fuel pipe from the pump to the carburettor is disconnected - it's pumping petrol straight into the engine bay and onto the hot exhaust pipe. We carefully reconnected it and looking dubiously at the wires many of which had their plastic insulation charred black by the fire had little confidence that it would run. Amazingly it started, so checking the brake light and indicators were still functioning I tentatively drove off with our escort behind watching for further conflagrations although with two empty fire extinguishers maybe throwing beer onto any conflagration would be all they could do.. We drove to the field on a farm between the coast and home where ironically we were meeting the others for a barbecue! We had really seen enough flames for the day but the food and drink was welcome. At home I had to replace much of the wiring loom in the engine compartment which thankfully in a 1960's VW camper is fairly rudimentary. And I must say

once the extinguisher powder was wiped away the engine bay looked cleaner than I had ever seen it with the flames having removed the residue of oil that normal covered much of the engine bay though its not a cleaning regime that I would recommendI am pleased to say that this was the most serious mishap in the campervan and considering its age and relative lack of technology it was reasonably well behaved.
Boyo - ready to go off camping.

For several summers running we drove it to a camp side above Chesil beach outside Weymouth and this trip normally tested the bus. One time we had only gone a mile down the road when some fault occurred. I think it was binding brake shoe so a visit to a friendly fellow club owner at his garage some three miles further fixed the problem after which we set off on the adventure and it did always seem an adventure travelling the hundred mile trip along the south coast. We usually broke the journey at a camp site in the New Forest which was a welcome stopover. Another time we only got as far as Littlehampton before some kind of fault forced an overnight stop with mechanical fettling. A favourite outing was to go further west from Weymouth to Lyme Regis, an outing enlivened by the long downhill stretch into the town which ended in a sharp bend to the right infant of the sea wall. It was possible to get up quite a speed, possibly 60 mph before fear, the knowledge of the brakes effectiveness and a dawning nightmare of failed brakes catapulting us through the sea wall and down onto the beach persuaded me to rapidly slow down. They say that what doesn't kill you makes you stronger but after one trip in modern rush hour traffic in the camper on the crowded M27 I vowed to stick to A and B roads. Another crowd pleaser was the summer when faulty starter motor required me to crawl underneath and hit or short the terminals bringing a shower of sparks while the co-pilot turned the starter whilst being helped by an excited collie worried that 50 percent of his 'flock' was being left behind. Yes, life is never dull in a camper van.

Entertainment was also provided for the co-pilot or maybe I should say one of the co-pilots as Boyo the collie cross would sit in the middle of the bench seat between us whilst S. had some ancillary duties one of which was to hold the passenger door with her left hand. I wasn't entirely sure that this was always necessary but as she had experienced the door flying open on one occasion when rounding tight ben she was convinced it was. In wet weather she was also deployed to mop up an drops of water that would enter the cab we think from the roof 'air box' above us that was some germanic early air flow system that would duct fresh air from above the windscreen into the cab trough vents above us. Unfortunately it also seemed to bring in water and on occasions small insects! Meanwhile I would be busy trying to see out, wrestling with the non-power steering, worrying about the poor braking ability and under acceleration, particularly up hills, holding the gear lever as it was known to occasionally jump out of gear. Yet I am saying it was one of my favourite vehicles and lamenting that I ever got rid of it.

I wasn't the only one. On arriving at one campsite and slowly driving to look for an empty pitch I was surprised to see an excited middle aged man running across the field towards us.

"I heard you arriving - the engine note is so nostalgic -my Dad had one like this and we went on holidays when I was a kid."

Slightly touched by his enthusiasm I asked if he would like to drive it the hundred yards or so across to the vacant pitches. He was like a kid at a funfair - he said it made his holiday and couldn't wait to tell his elderly Dad. He's probably gone out and bought one since and spends his weekends covered in oil and grease.

We collected another fan at that camp-site. We were awoken one morning by a metallic tapping that seemed to be coming from near the floor of the van. I got up and quickly got dressed as after peering out through the curtain I couldn't see anything outside that could be making the noise. Our dog was awake now and keen to get out so we both made our way across field to the cliff path before coming back to the camper. As we did we were hailed by the co-pilot who was standing head and shoulders out of the sunroof and saying the noise had come back. As I went around the other side of the camper, away from the awning on the side of the doors, I was met by the site of a very cross crow who was angrily pecking his reflection in the shiny, chrome, domed hubcap. His anger was rapidly mirrored by an uncharacteristically heroic lunge by Boyo who was indignant that this large black feather coated stranger should be vandalising his precious Bus. I have seen birds doing this before to hubcaps but the behaviour of our 'guard dog' dissuaded any further attacks on his during that holiday.

The small size of the camper van also brought a set of problems with it. My wife was nervous about sleeping with a gas bottle in the camper despite my reassurances that the regulator valve was securely turned off. "But what if it leaks or there's a fire and it explodes." So I would disconnect it every night and put it outside in the side awning some six foot or so away from the camper van. In the morning it would require reconnection before coff could be made but household paranoia of a conflagration involving bedclothes and the gas stove meant that the kettle couldn't be used until the bed had been put away, never mind the foam filled vinyl bed/seat cushions were still six inches from the gas ring. Anyway by this time the dog and myself had taken the air along the coastal path for a morning constitutional walk so we were both at least half awake and ready for breakfast. There was another concern for half the campers and that was a dread of waking up to have displayed a bare bum to the rest of the campsite by pressing it in sleep against the camper widow adjacent to the narrow bed. Personally, I avoided this fear by sleeping away from the window to selflessly shield others from exploding gas bottles. I am not sure the fear was fully justified and to this day don't know whether such a flash occurred or not. I do know that the roof height made it necessary to change clothes sitting down or lying on the floor until we discovered it was possible to stand up with head and shoulders out if the roof , smiling at passers by whilst removing or replacing any below the waist clothing unseen behind the curtains of the camper van. Oh yes camping provided all manner of unexpected entertainment.

More Madness

I had mentioned the tendency for classic cars to multiply. The normal way is for the prudent purchase of a second model of the same car to provide a secure source of spare parts as the original parts are shed or destroyed by rust on your forty year old vehicle. This wasn't my route to multiple ownership. I had always regretted the passing on of my white Volvo P1800 and had occasionally seen examples for sale in the classified ads of car magazines. One such ad caught my eye. This isn't the ad below but an earlier auction ad from the previous owner that I went to Hampshire to buy it from.

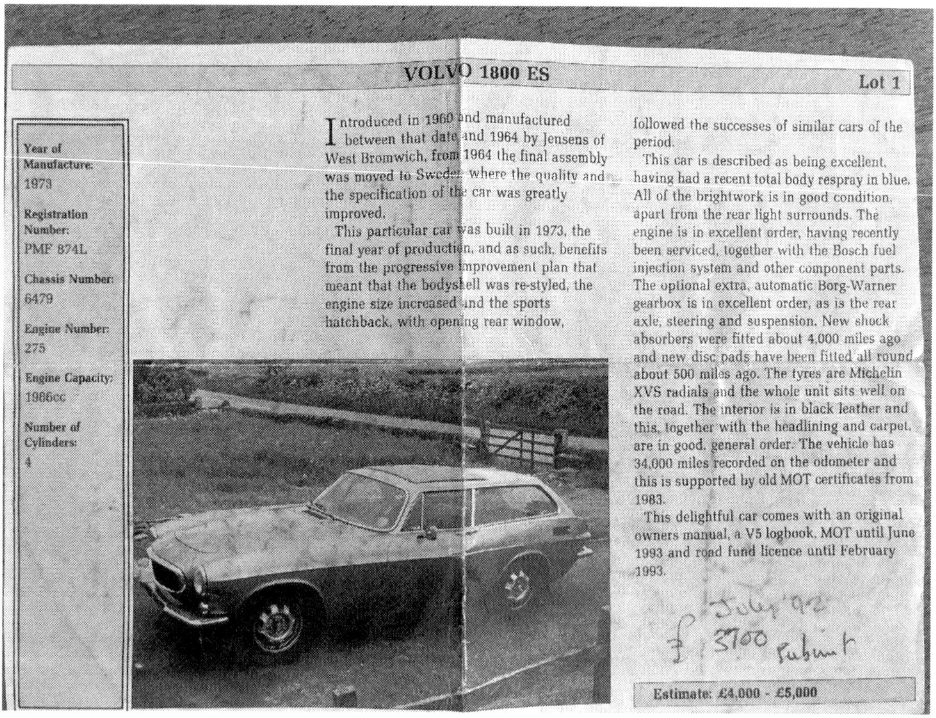

VOLVO 1800 ES — **Lot 1**

Year of Manufacture: 1973

Registration Number: PMF 874L

Chassis Number: 6479

Engine Number: 275

Engine Capacity: 1986cc

Number of Cylinders: 4

Introduced in 1960 and manufactured between that date and 1964 by Jensens of West Bromwich, from 1964 the final assembly was moved to Sweden where the quality and the specification of the car was greatly improved.

This particular car was built in 1973, the final year of production, and as such, benefits from the progressive improvement plan that meant that the bodyshell was re-styled, the engine size increased and the sports hatchback, with opening rear window, followed the successes of similar cars of the period.

This car is described as being excellent, having had a recent total body respray in blue. All of the brightwork is in good condition, apart from the rear light surrounds. The engine is in excellent order, having recently been serviced, together with the Bosch fuel injection system and other component parts. The optional extra, automatic Borg-Warner gearbox is in excellent order, as is the rear axle, steering and suspension. New shock absorbers were fitted about 4,000 miles ago and new disc pads have been fitted all round about 500 miles ago. The tyres are Michelin XVS radials and the whole unit sits well on the road. The interior is in black leather and this, together with the headlining and carpet, are in good, general order. The vehicle has 34,000 miles recorded on the odometer and this is supported by old MOT certificates from 1983.

This delightful car comes with an original owners manual, a V5 logbook, MOT until June 1993 and road fund licence until February 1993.

July '92
£ 3700

Estimate: £4,000 - £5,000

The car was the same model and colour, metallic blue, as the one that had given me a Mr Toad moment back in the early seventies on the seafront at Hythe in Kent (see the Triumph Herald chapter.) I had thought it wonderful then and still did all these years later. Whilst writing these memories I have trawled through old photos both pre-digital prints, scanned slides and more recent digital photo albums and although I haven't made a complete comparison, intuitively it appears that I have more photos of the two classic Volvos and the VW camper than of any other cars. In some cases the interiors were so anonymous that I haven't even recorded them but it suggests that these were the cars that held a special meaning to me. I would include the Alfa 156 in that category but although it was lovely to look at the best way to appreciate it was to drive it. The Triumph Spitfire has also become a latter day classic car and I am sorry that I don't have more photos of it. I have recorded details of the Avantime which due to it's eccentricity and rarity has also become a collectable modern classic so maybe its hard to judge which cars are destined for latter day fame.

The Volvo had a particular advantage because it's relative rarity meant that on a number of occasions when turning up to classic car shows we were allowed in free on condition that the car went in the exhibitors area. Sometimes I protested that I would have washed and polished it if I was expecting this but it was usually met with a kind comment of 'No, it's fine and we haven't got another like it in today.'

It was usually met on such occasions by puzzled comments from the public -'What is it ? A Volvo - it doesn't look like a Volvo.' This was true for the late 20th century Volvos were mostly boxy and sturdy looking in comparison to the flowing lines and chrome and curved glass of the 1800.

The other advantage the Volvo had as a classic car over the older VW bus was that it was perfectly fine to drive in modern traffic. It would drive at motorway speeds and good brakes meant that it wasn't the white knuckle drive of the VW and it seemed to still have Vovo's reputation for reliability. On most fridays I would drive it on the two hour round trip to the office unless I was in London or away. It also made a number of motorway journeys from Sussex to Swansea without incident. This compared favourably with the VW camper van's annual trips to Dorset via the New Forest which usually ended in some kind of roadside repair - but happily no fires.

The dash and instruments whilst interesting were rather plain after the 1967 P1800 Volvo which had a retro jukebox style going on as you can see below.

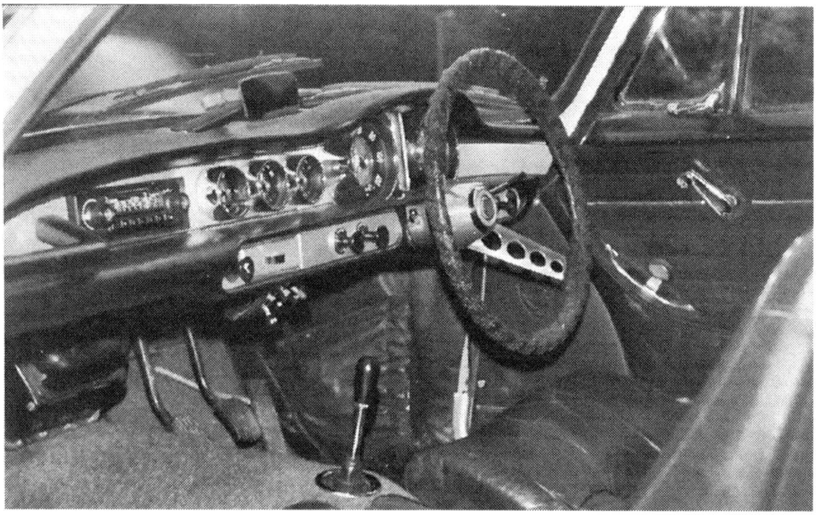

Owning a number of cars and occasionally arriving at the office would lead others to assume I was some kind of motoring and mechanical guru so would occasionally ask me technical questions (often beyond the extent of my knowledge) or else ask my opinion of certain cars when I would have to deploy uncharacteristic degrees of tact and diplomacy to disguise my true opinions. As in much of life I had the normal levels of prejudice often without any sound foundations. So would have to avoid saying what I might have thought such as only retired people should have Rover cars. Only farmers need 4 x 4's and most French cars are eccentric and generally horrible. These prejudices are of course rubbish and I have personally flouted them.
I was also accused, again by Arthur, of making one of the most swanky statements about cars that he had ever heard when I innocently announced that I like leather interiors and 'most of my cars had them.' I can see what he meant - I sounded like Jay Leno or Beaulieu Motor museum. I have often chosen cars on criteria of style but have been subjected to budgets or practical considerations assuming housing an Irish wolfhound is considered a practical consideration - I realise many would not. Are there cars I wish I had owned or still covet? I don't include the extreme exotica of lowly slung Bugatis or Ferraris although I did often think that owning a Maserati had a certain allure but I think I just like the word and they seemed less pretentious than other high end

marques so maybe a Maserati 3200 would be an exception - a mildly exotic Italian addition. With all of those there would be the worry of losing the front spoiler or sump on a speed bump or coming back to where you parked it to find it had been, damaged or vandalised out of jealousy. Even worse would be the worry that it wouldn't still be there but instead in a shipping container being 'exported' by international car thieves. The cars I might have liked to have owned are generally more prosaic and often just based on their looks. In no particular order they include with a vague attempt at rationales:-

Renault 4 - a boxy small French estate car enjoyed by Gallic farmers and country dwellers as a useful workhorse and less popular than the Citroen 2CV which always seemed to be excessively twee.

By the same token a more modern similar looking vehicle has a certain appeal - the Nissan Cube - mad Japanese styling - it even has a asymmetric rear window.

A second Japanese choice is the very practical but rather ugly Honda Element which wasn't released in the Uk but enjoyed US popularity as a leisure vehicle.
Another French choice - the space age Citroen DS with its sweeping lines and air suspension - style epitomised!
I have mentioned earlier my close brush with Welsh car ownership in the form of the Gilbern car company so the mustn't be forgotten.
As for Italian cars the Alfa Spider always appealed even though my Triumph Spitfire shared a resemblance. The later Alfa GTV looked stylish but when I drove one it seemed claustrophobic so maybe only in convertible

form. The original Land Rover Defender has appealed with its no nonsense basic go anywhere charm though the proper dull green colour rather lets its down sartorially and a white one would just show the dirt - maybe an airforce royal blue?
What were the other cars that appealed? German ones ? - strangely although I could see the appeal of the Audi TT the Audi that attracted me more was the clever aluminium original Audi A2 hatchback. I test drove one as a potential company car after the Alfa and although I liked it I was seduced by the more powerful Mercedes coupe thinking the Audi would be too pedestrian after the Alfa.

Around the same time we bought the Volvo ES I considered a 2 seater Mercedes SL 230 getting as far as sitting in one.
I had never desired a BMW having seen too many of them in my rear view mirror driven by overheated middle mangers in a rush towards their cardiac arrests. There have been two exceptions. The first was the electric I3 a cleverly packaged in BMW, the second is the M coupe that is a shooting brake style and I just like the look of it and it has a rarity bonus.

Probably my most unrealistic desire would be a Mercedes 300 SL -obviously with the double gull wing doors. I could never afford one but quite recently remember reading of someone using one as a very valuable every day driver. The idea that a mid 1950's production car with concept car design had similar performance to the 1990's Alfa (7 seconds to 60 - 140 mph.

When they first came out I was intrigued by the tiny 2 seater Smart car and eventually over a decade after their release we acquired one and still have it.
From the sublime to the ridiculous there was a time when owning a large but unloved saloon car at the time when they were beginning to be out of tune with the tastes of the time which had moved to people carriers and crossovers. Two of these that I momentarily considered were the futuristic and luxurious large Citroen C6 and the impressive VW Phaeton which was almost a disguised Bentley and claimed to be hand built and came with some incredibly powerful engines including a 6 litre W12! What they both shared in common was a very steep depreciation which gave them a bargain basement price (relatively.)
Probably for the best a number of factors stopped a serious consideration of getting either of these - firstly the less than happy ownership of the Avantime, also other demands on our bank balance, particularly the heap of stones on the Greek island, and maybe a dose of sanity for in the event this was the time I bought the Honda Jazz!
Do I still crave any eccentric cars - not at the moment although if VW pull their fingers out and get a modern electric VW split screen modern look alike into production I might be persuaded.

End of an Era

The ownership of the Alfa had given me the chance to try out other cars and marques with varying impressions. I wasn't to know it at the time but my next choice was to be my last company car. One car supplied to me while the Alfa was resting was a Mercedes saloon - a not particularly exciting one but I had been impressed with the comfort, power and build quality. So when it came the time to make my next choice I went into the Mercedes showroom in Sussex to look at the array of gleaming machinery on offer.
Among the wide choice of strange bulbous A classes and large saloons, estate cars and posing style convertibles was a new four seater two door hatchback coupe, simply named the C class Coupe. My wife had admired an S class coupe in another corner of the showroom and coming over to the one I was looking at that was some tens of thousands nearer the spending allowance my company was wasting on me. She immediately said this one's a better colour. So we sat in it, established the hatchback boot could accommodate our dog (without the need to try it as he wasn't of a wolf-hound's physique being a collie cross.)
The next week the garage was generous enough to lend me a demonstrator model overnight and I was impressed.
Performance felt sporty but more refined than the more aggressive Alfa which had a higher

power output and I suspect was lighter. Check-

ing this I find the kerb weights are 1330 Kg for the Alfa to 1480 Kg for the Mercedes and a higher bhp for the Alfa of 190 to 163. the sensation of speed was increased in the higher revving Italian by the exhaust noise. The engine in the Mercedes was a smaller 2.0 litre Kompressor petrol unit with the air to the engine being, I was told, 'supercharged.' Unfortunately the engine itself looked like a central heating boiler and was a let down after the Alfa visually but then the bonnet was only ever opened to top up the washers so the disappointment was infrequent. The photo below is from their brochure so they must been pleased with it.To reach my allocated budget I was able to specify a large electric glass roof which made the interior light. I also ordered the auto gearbox which unfortunately left no money for Mercedes very expensive leather

seats so these were a pleasant light grey mixture in cloth. I was shortly to regret this when a red wine bottle incident with the shopping left an embarrassing stain on the rear seat and caused a faulty seat belt warning message due to liquid getting to the sensor. The sympathetic dealer sorted both out and I think that was the sum total of mishaps in the car. In the photo below I am afraid I look a little smug - the car was attractive but less showy and less dangerous to drive than the Alfa and it didn't see to upset any of the company hierarchy by being in the company car park. It was to be my last company car and maybe in the final year of my employment I had conformed and chosen a dark colour german car like many others there - although it was a previously outlawed 2 door with a glass roof!

It was pleasant to drive, roomy for a coupe so that when I took early retirement I considered buying it off the company. The combination of a high residual value coupled with the knowledge it had been driven as a company car (see above about opening the bonnet to check the oil!) eventually persuaded me against this course of action.

Mercedes 300CE Coupe

I retired early and wasn't yet ready for a pensioners car and already having entered the dangerously seductive world of classic car ownership had started to research whether it was possible to own a future classic that would give the benefits of a modern vehicle. My conclusion was this dual purpose could be provided by a Mercedes 300 CE a large, pillarless coupe in a deep midnight blue metallic colour with a 3 litre 24 valve engine and uprated to include remote entry, alarm and cd multiplayer to add to the list of factory fitted extras. These included an electric steel sunroof, a full leather

interior, auto gearbox with traction control, headlamp washers, seatbelt arms that slid out electrically when the door was closed because of the lack of central pillar.
The car when new cost over £50 k which would be approx £90 k in present day money and its solidity and power felt like it. It cost me £5,000 and felt like a bargain. It was a fast and comfortable long distance cruiser we even had a holiday in France in it, something I never did in the the Espace.

The spec was impressive and for its time must have been close to the pinnacle of auto refinement. It couldn't be described as economical but that was the payback for the power and weight. The engine output was rated at 220 BHP with acceleration to 60 in under 8 seconds and a claimed top speed of 145 mph. It wasn't so popular with the rest of the household including the dog who slid around on the leather seats and wasn't impressed by the visibility of the coupe styling although the electric seatbelt seeds seemed to intrigue him. In retirement I was doing a little bit of consultancy work involving travel around the country so I was able to enjoy driving it without complaints from either of the passenger, canine or otherwise.

Gallic madness

My second car bought in retirement was an even rarer creature - a Renault Avantime. This has been quoted as an example of a concept car being put into production and quoted by others as the product of a rush of Gallic blood to the brain that should have been resisted.

In retrospect it was frankly quite bonkers but when I first saw one I wanted to own one and I am not really sure why. The concept was to create a four seater luxury tourer that was around the size and similar body shape, a teardrop monobloc, to the Renault Espace people carrier. But by lowering the suspension, in-

stalling a 3 litre six cylinder engine they had created an early sports utility vehicle.
The 'concept car' design included two large cantilever style doors that moved away from the car body before swinging open. The cabin was particularly light and airy with pillar- less side windows and two huge glass sunroofs, one of which opened and both able to be shielded by electric fabric blinds.

The idea of a pillar-less four seater with a large open sunroof may have been conceived for posing along the corniche in the South of France but the buffeting from the wind coupled with the ready availability of exhaust fumes on the roads in Sussex tempered the enjoyment of this. Although the global closing function where all four windows and roof would close at the single touch of button was a nice party trick. Similarly the choice of the engine giving 220 + bhp to the front wheels also gave a certain amount of excitement with the power being beyond the handing of the car. There was a claimed top speed of 140 mph which I think would be terrifying although it would be very tempting to overtake a low slung car on the autobahn at that speed whilst looking down through the large windows from your leather armchairs. The interior was as futuristic as the exterior with the dash board being relatively minimalistic. For the time, 2002, the car was luxurious and very well equipped with parking sensors, sat nav system, huge glass roof with electric blinds, cruise control, headlamp wash-

ers, electric heated seats in tan leather, climate control and a good music system.

The system was hidden behind a dampered lid and accepted multiple cd's which it swallowed one after another into the bowels of the car. Music could be controlled by the steering column or by a remote control handset! Very Gallic. All the controls were in odd places - the climate control near the front right hand side of the driver on the top of the dashboard with

a passenger override on the passenger side. The switches for the heated seats and door mirrors where both somewhere else and many of the controls and their positions didn't seem intuitive so that coupled with the surprising

power for such a high vehicle made the driving experience a strange one. Again as with some other cars I have acquired I like to think it was a bargain, When new it retailed at close to £30 k but after just three years the price had dropped like a stone to the £8 k I paid for it. I am afraid that at that time there were some inherent electrical problems with Renaults, namely the coil sets which appear to be fancy plug leads so that the car would occasionally shut down power to one cylinder and go into 'low power limp home mode.' Reading posts on the friendly Avantime owners forum revealed this to be a relatively common problem so much so that I carried a spare coil set in the car. After experiencing this three times myself I reluctantly felt that after less than two years

ownership the car had to go. It seemed a shame as it was the only other car that I had along with the Splitscreen VW that it was expected not to just wave to each other but to stop and have a conversation and this happened to me a couple of times. I am sure it would have also happened with the Volvo ES but I can't remember seeing another one whilst driving it. I guess with a total production world wide of some 6000 it was also unlikely. I was told that only 200 Avantimes were sold in the UK market so I was probably statistically unlikely to meet many.
I would like to say that the Avantime was the most eccentric and rarest mode of transport that I had owned but sadly this isn't true. It

was positively mainstream compared to The Caraboat!

I understand that the car was futuristic enough to be used in the Sci-Fi film 'Children of Men and some were destroyed in the production reducing the 200 total even more!

Going semi-Nautical

Nowadays hybrid vehicles are very fashionable but our hybrid was very much ahead of its time and in all honesty it probably still would be. This was a hybrid cabin cruiser boat / caravan made of fibreglass on a metal chassis with two wheels and an inboard petrol jet engine! Allegedly the idea of a marine architect in Nottingham, launched on an unsuspecting public in 1973 (the era of hovercrafts and amphicars) and according to legend the subject of a disastrous PR exercise at the launch. The story goes that due to the strength of the river flow and the lack of power in the engine a party of local dignitaries including the mayor had to be rescued to avoid being swept over a weir and risking drowning. It is thought only some 60 odd were made before the embarrassed inventor smashed up the moulds - and yes we bought one. In my defence I would say :-

a. it was cheap
b. I had only owned a rowing boat on our pond up to this acquisition
c. We already had a camper van and this seemed a logical development
d. when sanity prevailed after only a bit of cleaning I sold it for a £500 profit.

So how did this come about - blame the internet! We were out for a day near Bodiam castle not far from our home in East Sussex when on a river near the pub garden where we were having lunch we saw a sweet little cabin cruiser, Someone in the bar commented it was used by a local minister who said between two churches. I was never able to establish the truth of this but was entranced by the idea if a small river boat -probably another 'Toad of Toad Hall moment.' A trawl of boats for sale came up with a Caraboat for sale and restoration on the River Trent near Nottingham. A subsequent internet search revealed an active Caraboat owner's forum complete with helpful hints on restoration and seductive photos of comfy interiors with kitchens and adaptable sofa beds and folding tables of the sort we were familiar with from our caravans and camper van. Coincidentally, we were due to stay with a friend not far away so I took the plunge and phoned the owner. He said it was moored on the river and described it as a partial restoration project but if we went to see it and we were still interested he could arrange delivery to the south of England. Some days later we found ourselves on the banks of the river Trent viewing the abandoned boating rarity. The seller was not available but had sent some photos to help us locate it and recognise it although recognition wasn't so much of a problem there was nothing else like it. It wasn't moored on an official jetty but tethered to a tree and although afloat we could see some water and god knows what else inside it. So back at home I found myself a few days later phoning the owner and saying having seen it we were still interested but would getting it to East Sussex present any problems and what would it cost. This would be no problem and he had someone who could deliver as

he wasn't available as it was his busy season. But for an all in price of £250 we would become the new owners and the boat would be brought to Sussex. I then made the mistake of asking what he did that made him so busy in the summer. The reply shocked me :-
"I am professional clown!" he said with a certain amount of undisguised pride.
We had bought a boat with wheels, full of water and mud some 200 plus miles away from a CLOWN !
I spent the next few days before the agreed delivery date researching things Caraboat. The small group of owners were a helpful resource about the history of the craft and hints and details about the restoration process. One enthusiast even sent me a dvd of the restoration

process of his own craft. All of these made me even keener for our own 'dreamboat' to arrive. There was a rather curious phone call from the 'Clown's Friend' aka the delivery man the day before the agreed date which should have set some alarm bells ringing.
"I am planning to leave Nottingham very early tomorrow morning so should be with you around 9 -ish."
'Great no problem -you have the email with local directions for our house? You can always phone when nearby and I can direct you.'
"Yes, thanks - I have one question -Are you south or north of London?"
A little shocked - I explained East Sussex was south of London and described the junction number they would need to leave the M25 from.
"Yes - I have heard of the M25 - is it a motorway? - I am sure we'll find you - see you tomorrow morning."
And he was gone.
I cynically commented that it sounded like our boat vendor had recruited one of the other clowns from the circus for the delivery but hoped I was joking.
The next morning 9 o'clock came and went. So did 10 o'clock and 11 o'clock and I eagerly listened to the 12 o'clock radio news bulletin to see if there were any reports of a shutdown of any southbound carriageways on the motorway network due to a hybrid boat/ caravan vehicle incident. At last around 12.30 the phone went -

"Hello, it's Bob delivering your boat. It's taking longer than I thought. We've been over the large bridge and through the toll tunnel and now we see signs to the airport -Is that near you? - We forgot to bring our road atlas."
'yes - signs to Gatwick airport?" you need to leave the M25 at the junction for the A21 sign-posted to Hastings.'
"No, the airport is Stanstead."
'WHAT - you are going north!'
"But we can't be - we crossed the Thames on the bridge."
'Yes but somehow you crossed it again by using the tunnel - I don't know how - did you leave the motorway somewhere after the bridge.'
"There were some roadworks and we got confused - I don't really know - so we don't go to Stanstead airport then?"
'Er - no, you need to turn off at the next junction and come back onto the motorway to go south.'
Inspiration kicked in -
'Is it sunny there - it is here - you need to go south -towards the sun. Call again when you leave the motorway and you are on the A21 and I will drive out and look out for you and lead you back.'
This plan seem to have a flaw as far as the clown/driver was concerned.
"Yes but how will I recognise you ?"
-'YOU WON'T NEED TO ! I will spot you there won't be any other Caraboats being towed on

the English road network today - I am prepared to risk that.'
I cheered myself up by imagining the scenes in the rooms where the motorway cameras are monitored - "There's that weird caravan boat thing again" - or maybe "there's another of those weird boat caravan things - that's the third or fourth today - never seen one before!"
I was phoned to be told the deliverers were now on the A21 and still had their controls 'Set for the Heart of the Sun' just like the early Pink Floyd release. I left for the planned interception leaving the gate to the drive open to allow the hoped for vehicle/trailer/boat/caravan imminent arrival and hoping to avoid a multiple vehicle /boat/ trailer/caravan shunt whilst I stopped to open the gate on my return.
The rendezvous went surprisingly smoothly. The car trailer Caraboat combination was spotted by me from the lay-by where I had parked and phoning to confirm I was able to overtake on the next straight and lead them the few miles back home. After the drama of the proceeding few hours the drop off was straightforward and the delivery man left refusing our offer of refreshment and before I could pluck up the courage to confirm his clown credentials. We were now the proud owners of a Caraboat restoration project including a generous helping of River Trent mud which covered the floor and some of the lower walls of the cabin.
For the first few weeks the activity was restricted to clearing out the mud and generally

cleaning off the dirt and mould so we could have a proper look at the task ahead. I have copied below some extracts from the original brochures from the early 1970's which together with other material from the enthusiasts of the Caraboat Owners group should have spurred us on with the restoration.

Next using a jet wash we were able to strip off the green paint to reveal the yellow self coloured fibre glass and the remnants of an old name transfer giving the craft the glorious name of Hippo which seemed to accurately fit its top heavy bulbous form. The jet wash and the volume of water at least proved that the hull was water tight as it needed to dry out or be baled out. The original brochure and

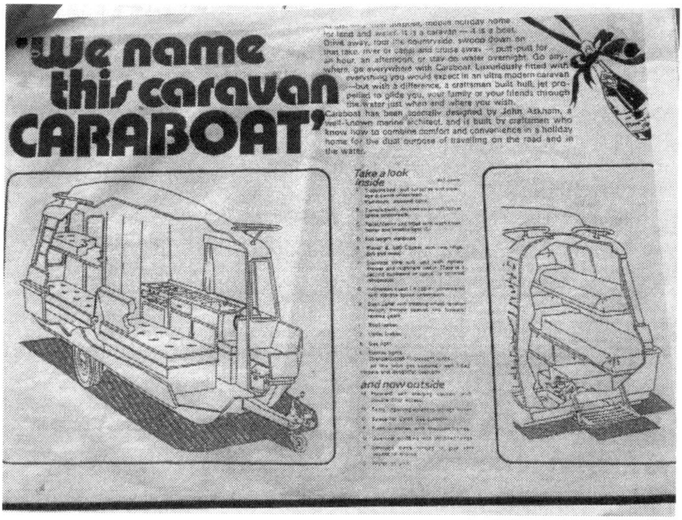

restoration dvd showed a large expanse of glass but most of the panels had been replaced on ours either by ply wood or frosted glass. Taking a piece of ply out of one of the panels towards the front or bow as us boat owners call it revealed the aluminium frame to be in

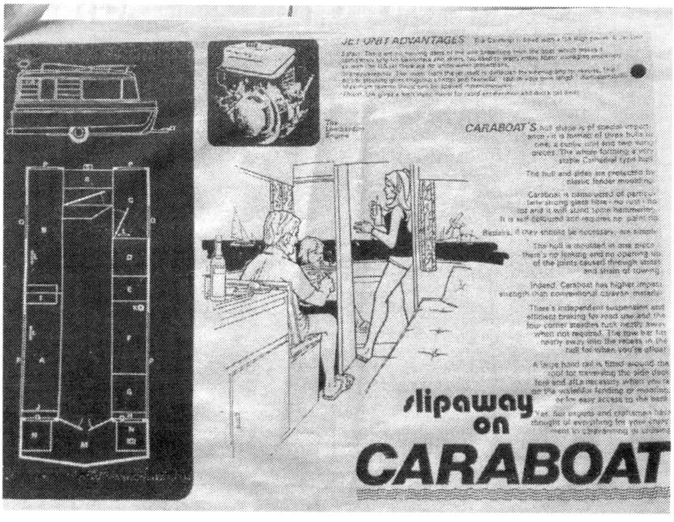

good condition once the mastic was laboriously scraped out. We felt cleaning and restoring the upper part of the boat (or caravan ?) to be possible for us but the restoration hints from other owners suggested reinstalling the tow bar and arranging a secure fitting for the necessary outboard motor plus arranging the controls to be placed near the bow to be quite a specialised task. On top of this was the question of the wheels and drum brakes necessary for the caravan (boat?) to be towed. This was definitely work for another day. We had already fitted out our VW camper van with a camping interior comprising storage cupboards, a rock and roll convertible bed, sink with pumped water, small gas cooker and fridge, plus folding seats and tables so the interior fittings were felt to be within our skill-set.
I am not sure what it was that exactly brought our plans of restoration to a halt. Maybe I have insufficient nautical aspirations. Apart from a few ferry trips, a couple of dinghy sailing trips with friends and some wind surfing lessons my water going experience was mostly like the London power station : Bankside. It may have been the commitment to a country garden of a few acres that occupied much of our free time coupled with the ownership I already had of two other motoring rarities and keeping them running, namely the 1966 VW Splitscreen camper van and the 73 Volvo 1800ES.

Having come to a decision about abandoning the project the next task was to sell it. Al-

though the Caraboat owners forum had been a welcome source of information it seemed that for all of them the ownership of one Caraboat was sufficient. Maybe their trials and tribulations of restoration and ownership had also deterred their friends - or maybe they were so eccentric to not have any friends - who knows? The conclusion was to put it on Ebay though there was some debate which category to use - Boat / Caravan or Caravan / Boat ? I think I must have used both. Not surprisingly it was the only one on there - worldwide !
Deciding not to be greedy I put it up with an opening bid at price that I had bought it for £ 150. I was reasonably experienced in using eBay both for buying and selling so I wasn't surprised that I didn't receive any bids for the first half of the week but I was pleasantly surprised how many viewings it got - in the high hundreds. There were also a healthy number of watchers over 50 after four days but I am sure many of these clicked on 'watch' to show their partner or colleague later who may have dismissed a verbal description as some type of hallucination. Still whatever happened at least we wouldn't have to wrap it up.
I mention this as I had around the same time I had unwisely expressed some outrage at a Sussex auction house that had severely disappointed an elderly friend of a friend by selling a large and precious (to her) bone china dinner service and achieved a grand total for her after commission of some £ 30 ! Our friend, Yvonne was upset on her behalf particularly as she was

contemplating doing the same with her Royal Doulton service she had collected but admitted it would break her heart to get so little for something she had collected over the years at far greater expense. I had rashly said that I believed it would be much more profitably to list it piecemeal on Ebay where collectors could add to their collections. The commitment made, there followed a programme of photographing dozens of pieces and inputting individual listings of tea plates, gravy boats and serving dishes and a lot more. This was followed by some exciting end of auction bidding and Yvonne's joy at the idea that two of her dinner plates were off to Canada or Holland. The most onerous part was the wrapping parties that seemed to take hours and a lot of bubble wrap but it was all worth it when the auctions netted over £350 for her. There was a poignant moment when she said that although she was pleased with the sales she wished she'd just kept a couple of things. Luckily being experienced in the vagaries of human nature we had held back couple of what I think are called Trios, a cup, saucer and plate plus a small jug. This she said was the icing on the cake!

Anyway there was no way we were keeping any souvenirs of the Caraboat - we had only just distributed the River Trent mud in the hedge. On the day of the auction end the number of views and watchers escalated again and by the time we sat down to watch the last twenty minutes before it ended, with a glass

each to calm us, the numbers kept climbing and new bids came in. At first it climbed slowly £160, 165, 175... £200. Then maybe some of the bidders were also fortified with drinks - the bids started to climb in £50 increments with a last minute flurry during the 30 second countdown to achieve £750 - brilliant!
The following week the buyer arrived and it was trailered back to the Midlands - it was going home.
Out of curiosity I googled Caraboat at the time of writing and one had been offered in 2020 for completion at offers around £3500 described as one of the last dozen in existence - anyone tempted? Then I found another one that had

been restored that ended the auction unsold but with a starting price of £14500 !

Wise Choice

I can credit my wife for my next acquisition which was a more mainstream and perhaps appropriate one as they are considered widely to be pensioner's vehicles. We had already exchanged the Suzuki for a different car for her as some electrical issues had questioned its reliability. The replacement vehicle wasn't chosen in the way that I do with visits to showrooms, car magazine reviews or scrutinising member club forms. No - she noticed a car in a pub car park in one of our nearby villages and said "what's that - I like the look of it." It was a Honda HRV that we were later to discover had been launched with the unlikely but aspirational slogan of 'Joy Machine!'
We were unaware of that at the time and might have put us off. I replied that it was a Honda - they were known to be reliable and were generally relatively more expensive than similar more common cars. That must have inspired her for not long afterwards she found a good example, a couple of years old in a garage in the next town. I was phoned and told the trade in price for the ailing Vitara that had been offered without the garage examining it so she bought it. When it arrived it did have the legend "HRV joy machine" written on the boot lid, admittedly in relatively discreet and small letters. The HRV was an early example of what has become known as a 'crossover' and Honda used the initials from the term 'High Ride Vehicle.'

I am afraid we took this car for granted as it was completely reliable needing little attention apart from disposable items such as tyres and brake pads etc. It was serviced infrequently and always passed MOT's first time so consequently it remained a family friend for almost ten years and was only sold when we moved to a city and assumed we would only need one car. On several occasions we briefly lent it to friends who were in between cars for a short time and they were always surprised how nice it was to drive. A high driving position, a very smooth gearbox and simple controls. The engine was powerful enough without being aggressive and it just seemed a no-nonsense package. The trusty car was such an anonymous part of our lives that I can't really find any decent photos of it. To prove this fact here

is one of the best photos of it as a walk on bit player while photographing another car's flashier interior.

The second photo is from the HRV brochure and seems to confirm the company's stated aim of trying to reach out to a younger demographic with this model. I am not sure how successful this aspiration was, at least in the UK where Honda was traditionally seen as appealing to older and maybe more astute owners interested in reliability. Interestingly while we owned it we frequently travelled to the

Greek island of Crete were indeed the car was usually seen being driven by cool looking 20's and 30 year olds. My wife would say that she always knew it was a cool.

The actual production model was not too dissimilar to the original concept

Here it is again ready to start first time as always - not always a certainty for the first two decades of my car ownership. You still see a few in rural areas in everyday use despite being out of production now for 15 years. I remember reading survey in 2011 which I have just checked again on the internet which listed the most reliable used 4 x 4's and topping the list was the Honda HRV followed by a Suzuki Vitara. Thus proving if you want reliable advice on cars don't speak to me but speak to my wife. (I am told that this also applies to many other forms of advice outside the scope of this book!)

A Period of Sanity (at least Car-wise.)

Some time in the summer of 2008 I had something of a car epiphany. It was the culmination of a number of events not all car related. The Avantime's electrical faults with the coil sets had been annoying me for some time and I was unhappy with the lack of reliability in what was a modern supposedly prestige car. The Volvo ES had been off the road for some time due to braking system problems that were beyond my expertise (and the first mechanic who tried to sort it out.) It seemed it would need costly specialist attention and had been sitting under a car cover for over a year already. The beloved VW camper van had failed the last MOT with a lot of expensive welding work required. It was a couple of years since we completed our fifth VW London to Brighton run and the last camping week in Dorset had proved to require more mechanical mucking about on the car than made for a restful trip. In the course of a week I had sold the Volvo to a classic car enthusiast who was shipping it home to Sweden. The Chairman of the Sussex VW club who ran a business restoring VW's bought the camper from me and later that year undertook a long and expensive restoration process on it thus saving it. Surprisingly it was the only car I had ever owned that I sold for more than I originally paid for it despite the work required. The Split screens have continued to increase in value but will still require investment to keep roadworthy and I found in

the later years of ownership that it was becoming much less pleasurable driving in modern traffic with other drivers impervious to the stopping capabilities of a thirty year old design with all round drum brakes and no air bags!
The Avantime was traded in at the local Honda dealer (their initial reaction was what the hell is it?)
I had caved in and acquired a sensible car - a pensioners car - A 'Flippin' Honda Jazz hatchback.
Our lives were not completely boring - we were several years into the restoration of an ancient stone village house on the Greek island of Crete and were getting regular building bills from the architect there who was (slowly) managing the restoration.

The story of this can be followed in my earlier book for sale on Amazon - "A Small House in Crete."
This fact combined with increasing frustrations of old cars led to this drastic act so that in one week we went from a four car household to a two car one - both Hondas!

A surprising revelation! In many ways the little Honda was the best car I had ever owned - really! It did everything that was asked of it. We drove tens of thousands of miles in it without incident. It was economical, fine at motorway speeds and seemed impossibly bigger on the inside than the outside. It was well equipped for the time with electric mirrors, windows and sun roof, air conditioning. Instrumentation was pretty simple but included what i thought of as the 'smugmeter' which read out the average mpg. As we did limited urban driving it consistently read in the mid 40's mpg. It always passed its MOT without any problems and servicing was good value at the local Honda dealer, a family company. The only mild surprise was when I noticed on a service invoice that 8 spark plugs had been replaced. It appears that the engine was a twin spark design something that Alfa Romeo and others cite as designed to enhance power and performance two characteristics that were not part of the Jazz repertoire. What it did provide was brilliant economy though the car wasn't sluggish. It did provide entertainment of a different sort when I would drive up to collect a large item probably bought at an auction or on eBay to be told 'don't think it'll fit in there mate!' for me to demonstrate that by the rear seats folding flat to the floor and sometimes flattening the back of the passenger seat too - that indeed it will fit in there - mate! I had usually prepared by carefully measuring the space against the stated dimensions of the item but in popular estate agent jargon the Jazz was 'deceptively spacious.' This capacity was recognised by an old friend of mine who had been a big fish in the advertising industry - Bruce had christened one that was owned in their family - 'The Tardis' being apparently bigger inside than on the outside ! The previously enjoyed reliability was tested on day when a suspicious noise on the car when it was some six years old made me suspect an exhaust or manifold leak but then I realised it was varying at speed which pointed to something between the wheels and the drive shafts. A call to the friendly local Honda dealer confirmed this with the staggering statement of 'we've never replaced an exhaust on a Jazz so I don't think it can be that so if you bring it in we'll have a look.' He was right, a quick test run and he concluded a worn wheel bearing was the likely fault and the good news was that any Honda whatever age with this fault had the replacement, parts and labour, free of charge and the icing on the cake was when he told me the bill that I didn't need to pay would have been some £250. Now that's good customer service.

Apart from new tyres and normal servicing this turned out to be the only repair in some five years of ownership.

I am concluding that modern cars are generally less exciting and reviews seem to confirm this with as much attention being paid in column inches to the ease of use of the sat nav or sound system as the engines characteristics. Maybe reliability comes at a price and that price is blandness and loss of drama or funny motoring anecdotes.

When you always expect a car to start or work flawlessly any departure is viewed with frustration and a call to AA Relay rather than the old fashioned exercise of mechanical expertise, qualified or otherwise. Recent faults in new cars have only resulted in the relevant warranty man running up and plugging in a laptop then saying "Ah yes, fault code xyz = we better take the car to the dealer. I am not sure they now understand what is going on under the bonnet than I do. One such visit to see the Smart car when it was misbehaving started with a puzzled search for the engine (it's in the back under the boot,) followed by a second search for the car battery (in the front at the back of the passenger's footwell.) Both discoveries seemed to be news to the mobile expert mechanic!

The ignorance is also duplicated in the car showrooms. When the new Mini i.e. BMW appeared in the showroom I asked a fresh faced young sales man about the engine of this so called retro styled car. He proudly told me it

was 1.6 petrol. To which I added "fuel injection?"
To my amazement he said 'No, I don't think so.'
I was having fun now - so my reply of "You mean it's got carburettors - isn't that taking retro stying a bit far."
I left chuckling before I took more amusement by asking him to open the bonnet to check. I fear he probably wouldn't have known how to. Perhaps the move to electric cars is a natural progression of this and such designs will be simpler and more like when as a child I prised the body off a toy car and managed to replace one of the axles with a small electric motor, connect a battery and watch it fly across the bedroom and make an interesting mark on the paintwork on the skirting board which was to later mystify my Dad when he was redecorating.

Two New Cars

We were concerned that the trusty Honda HRV was getting a little long in the tooth so intended keeping the newer Jazz until we chose a replacement. The move to Wales was a move back to my home city that I had left after graduating many years before and never expecting to live in again. Not that I had anything against it and we had returned frequently even after my parents, who had also retired back there but had now passed away. We had spent time in our holiday home on the coast in Crete and had concluded that being isolated with the dual commitment of a huge garden and an ancient draughty and high maintenance house was something that we would need to change sooner rather than later. We had always embraced changes in our lives and would rather make any change rather than have it imposed on us. So we had started to look around, initially in Sussex to see where we could move to. Once issues of workplace or family are no longer in the equation the choice becomes almost too large. I won't be disrespectful to any of the Sussex locations that we considered, just to say none of them seemed to provide what we thought we wanted from a move. Some people when they retire make a move to a town or resort that they had previously only holidayed at and that can work but in a sense we had already done that with our little holiday home on Crete. We knew we were looking for a less remote location as we no longer wanted a five or six mile round trip to buy milk or further for many other things. The nearest palatable country pub for a lunch or supper meant a fifteen minute drive in each direction and this wasn't going to change. One a visit back to Swansea my wife suddenly said "What about Swansea - have you considered living here again?"

My gut reaction was -'No - I never thought I would move back.' There was no logic to that - just it had been forty years - I had left to go away to university and apart from a couple of months after graduating and having a holiday job before moving to Kent for my first proper job, I hadn't lived or worked in the city. Considering what it had to offer all in all it didn't seem a bad choice and once we found some new build developments on waterfront brownfield sites the option became attractive to us. The house we chose was within walking distance of both the coastal path and the city centre so going to one car seemed a practical option but of course it wasn't the option we chose. Within a month of moving we had traded in the Jazz for a nearly new 4 x 4 and had taken out a lease on a new Smart car - ideal for the city. This was the logic - a comfortable larger car for going away and trips to the airport and a small city car for local use.

The Smart car acquisition was a new one to us as we decided to take it as a lease with a purchase option.

There were a couple in stock in our local Mercedes dealer and not having researched the car

I was pretty amazed by the refinement - Air con, sat nav, cd, dvd & phone hands free, glass roof, electric mirrors and automatic gearbox with paddle controls on the steering wheel. Having said that, it wasn't exactly cheap for it's size but then in a Mercedes dealer it seemed small change. My wife was as sold on the idea and I must admit it seemed revolutionary and unlike anything we had ever owned before. The one she chose was in a matt grey with black highlights and the test drive pleased both of

us.
The pleasure of ownership of this brand new little spaceship was sadly short-lived as after only a month or so it started having intermittent electrical faults which either put it into 'limp home' mode or required actual recovery.

The dealer returned it to us each time having' fixed' the problem only for it to reoccur much to our annoyance.
It was only when it was returned to the dealer for the fourth or fifth time that we insisted that they drove it after the next 'fix' until the fault occurred. Happily for us but not for him, this was when the workshop manager was using it for his fifty mile drive home. At last we were believed that the car had a serious problem and meeting with the Dealership supremo over coffee and biscuits resulted in an agreement to replace the car. I don't know whether the fact it was a lease made any difference to this but the sad saga didn't end there. We were given a list of similar vehicles available through their national network and sensing we now had the upper hand insisted on one with an equivalent spec which was currently in a dealership on the Isle of Wight. We were told we could hang onto the loan vehicle - one of several we had used over the couple of months while we were trying to convince the garage there was some

major fault inside the 'brain' of ours and awaited notice of the new car.
It was not straightforward as the next phone call a few days later told us without a hint of humour that the replacement car had fallen of the transporter whilst being loaded onto the IOW ferry. We didn't know whether to laugh or cry but decided we would go into the dealer again as the base model Smart on loan lacked power steering which despite its size made parking more onerous than with power steering. Before we visited the dealer the sales person who we had originally dealt with us phoned while we were returning from a rare bike ride.
"Would we like to see a car close to our spec in the showroom?"
Checking with them, a little tongue in cheek, that it hadn't fallen off the back of a lorry we agreed that we would come straight over.
She quickly added "there may be one problem - where your last car was black this one is bright red ....but the main colour is the same matt grey."
When we arrived I couldn't help thinking of Starsky and Hutch - see what I mean overleaf !

The spec was similar to the original one but substituted heated seats instead of electric mirrors and to our relief the flappy paddle change had gone which neither of us liked. The new Smart has been reliable so the first one just must have been a rogue one. It's great for parking, no road tax and very infrequent visits to filling stations. We are always surprised how many similar ones we see in Southern European countries, Lisbon, Rome and Malta was packed with them.

Evocation

Turning to the second car we acquired on my return to Wales, no it wasn't a Gilbern although the museum had one on show at a Welsh manufacturing display. No this was to be the car for longer distances and when the Smart didn't have enough seats or luggage space. Of course the heart ruled the head and instead of buying a new, sensible Honda we started looking at the new design led Range Rover Evoque released the previous year and praised for looking unlike anything else. The local Land Rover dealer was helpful and took us for a test drive in a demonstrator which seemed as nice to travel in and drive as it looked. I was now contemplating spending the largest sum of my own money on a car that we had only previously and casually admired as a good design. We nearly backed out of buying one as we were told of a waiting list of up to six months. The young sales guy asked if we would consider a nearly new or ex-demonstrator that they could try and source nationally. So I found myself drawing up a rough list of requirements, a diesel engine, auto gearbox, a light interior and ideally a colour rather than black or silver. A couple of days later the dealer called to say that they had details of a low mileage Evoque, less than a year old that they could have brought from a Milton Keynes for us to look at with no obligation. They would email me the details and I could let them know if I was interested.

The car when seen mostly met my list of requirements apart from the light interior - inside a lot of it was black with thick comfy black leather seats this was compounded by dark privacy glass that would have given a gangster vibe to the car if it had been black, thankfully it was metallic red. To compensate it came with a large glass, panoramic roof that did compensate for the dark upholstery. It was described as a 2.2 SD4 Pure (tech) auto. I've said it before but who dreams up these catchy names.

Technical stuff:- the brochure tells me the SD4 has an 190 bhp output, 121 top speed, 0-60

time of 8 seconds, combined mpg claim of 43.5.
I loved the look of it, liked the power and performance and it was so quiet inside you were unaware it was a diesel but I was a little over awed by the technology. It was packed with it and their acronyms and to quote the brochure there were:-
DPF (Diesel particulate filter)
ABS (Anti lock brakes)
EBA (not the auction site but Emergency brake assist)
ETC (4 wheel traction assist)
DSC (Dynamic stability control)
HDC (Hill descent control)
RSC (not the Royal Shakespeare company but Roll stability control)
EPD (Electric parking brake)
Terrain Response ?
HLA (Hill launch assist)
And probably some other acronyms I never found out about.
Assuming most of these would be taken care of by the car's brain I now started to familiarise myself with what was expected of me. Firstly there was the keyless ignition, as long as the key for the car was in your pocket you could open the car and start it by pressing the starter button. All very good but the salesman issued a warning citing another customer who was driven the twenty or so miles to the garage after their partner had started the car at home but then got out and when the 'keyless' driver stopped the car and got out the

garage had no way of restarting the car until the key was retrieved from home. Technology - huh!

Much of the information was conveyed through two dash screens. One in front of the driver between the speedo and rev counter, the other large one in the centre of the dash which showed the sat nav screen.

Using the car choosing criteria mentioned a few decades before by a friend - the seats were very comfortable and supportive, adjustable and heated. Similarly there was a high quality 380 watt Meridian hi-fi system with ten speakers! The most frequently commented on feature was the silhouette of an Evoque which appeared illuminated at the door side at night when the car was unlocked, projected from under the side mirrors. A gimmick but very cool. The complexity of the controls on the car did cause some slight alarm to me on two separate occasions. The first was when trying to do something else, I don't recall what, when I inadvertently engaged the previously mentioned HDC or Hill Descent Control. Unlike when Captain Kirk tells the crew of the Starship Enterprise to engage warp drive the car had the opposite reaction and lurched to a crawl, having changed down several gears and pressing the accelerator didn't seem to achieve much apart from raising the engine note. Fortunately, there wasn't a car behind me too rear end me as I don't know whether the brake lights had shown and as soon as a I saw the HDC

Engaged message showing helpfully in the dash I knew I had caused something to happen. Quite what I didn't know until I had pulled over, rooted out the thick handbook from the glove box and found HDC in the index and also found the button to disengage it. I have never touched the button again.
I guess in many ways the car was over-engineered for my purposes and I didn't exploit it's potential such as its stated ability to 'Wade water' up to half a metre deep. I think I drove through a shallow ford, once.
The permanent four wheel drive felt safe on the road but I only intentionally used the snow setting a few times - well we lived on the coast in balmy South Wales not Iceland.
The second minor drama was when taking a passenger somewhere when they reached across to one of the set of control buttons by the gear selector and started stabbing at a number of them. I was alerted to this by the handling of the car changing and a series of icons flashing across the info screen on the dash including a Tree, a Cactus and Snowflakes. When I realised the cause - I exclaimed with mounting annoyance - "What the hell are you doing ! Your changing the car settings to sand, mud or snow."
She replied - 'Just trying to open my window..that's how you do it on my car' - the remainder of the journey was relatively silent. Thank god she hadn't turned on the HDC.

I don’t really want to rant about the frustrations of modern technology as much of it is a boon to our lives and we would now be lost with many conveniences that it provides. Unfortunately our reliability experiences with these two modern cars did cause us some frustration.

The Evoque also developed an intermittent ‘brain problem’ displaying an engine fault warning light and going into limp home mode. It was eventually traced to a faulty turbo unit that had to be completely replaced at great expense but fortunately under manufacturers warranty so the joy of initial ownership was somewhat compromised. Once our faith was restored in it we used it for many long and comfortable journeys.

An accidental buy?

When I had company cars I would sometimes get invitations by dealerships to the launch of their latest models which would often be an opportunity to have your appetite whetted by new cars outside your price range. The Land Rover dealer shared their premises with Jaguar cars so I wasn't surprised to receive an invite to the launch of their new Jaguar car - the confusingly named E-Pace, confusing as it wasn't electric - their electric car is the I-Pace! I must have liked it as I have a photo of the launch car shown here. I even sat it and admired the interior that seemed more car-like than the Evoque. Conversation with the sales staff wasn't convincing enough for me to think about raiding our bank account as I asked what the Jaguar had that I didn't already have in my four year old Evoque. The difference mainly seemed in marginally better mpg due to the four wheel drive switching in and out when required rather than permanent and a suite of driver assistance features.
Also the price of the top of the range model on display was pretty eye watering.
I left the showroom and quickly forgot about the Jaguar and it was only early in 2019 that having read positive reviews of the Volvo that I started to consider

changing the Evoque. We had owned four Volvos previously so maybe this was my brand loyalty resurfacing. A visit to the local Volvo dealer proved unsatisfactory. The car had been launched in 2017 but the dealer had no demonstrators or pre-owned that I was able to drive and the only one on the dealership was a manual and recent experience of city driving in the Range Rover and Smart car made me reluctant to consider a manual again.
The order book was some months out and I was reluctant to order any car that I hadn't driven.
On the way home we passed the Land Rover/ Jaguar dealer and on a whim I suggested we look at their stock and as

we parked I saw an E-Pace on the forecourt in an unusual colour, somewhere between grey and putty or new plaster. "That one looks good, an unusual colour" said my wife who always chooses anything based on colour and design aesthetics. Within minutes we were sitting inside it. Described by the keen sales person as a top of the range, year old, ex demonstrator with only 8000 odd miles on the clock the interesting paint colour was nicely complemented by a light oyster (their description), leather interior and a panoramic glass roof that lightened the interior.

The test drive only confirmed the impression of a sportier drivers car even though the test data for the vehicle was similar to the figures for the Evoque. I guess we were sold as soon as we saw it on the forecourt and there was some upside with one years depreciation it was a better price than the one at the launch that I had seen. As they say - you can't take it with you so we bought it, part exchanging the Evoque, now five years old. So after a gap of some thirty six years I was once again a Jaguar driver albeit a British design, manufactured in Austria by an Indian owned company.

The car like many today seems overloaded with technology some of which is useful, some distracting and some just to complex to bother getting to grips with. I had first hand experience of this the first time I drove it in traffic when bleeping and a big red indicator on the dash told me I was too near the car in front and the car was taking matters into its own hands and braking. I momentarily took my eyes of the car in front to try and understand what the light was. I guess the car would stop me driving into the car in front but the violence of the braking made me worry about being rear-ended. Fortunately this didn't happen but as soon as I could find out how I switched off the 'Robot nanny emergency brake.'

Buying a modern car is now akin to buying a computer on four wheels and its not a welcome trend.

At least I liked the appearance of the Jaguar and driving it has more of an engaging feel than any of the recent cars I have owned.

Of the technology there are some things I like and find useful:-
-the electric assisted tailgate,
-the electric adjustable front seats with memory setting
-auto lights with auto headlamp dipping
-parking warning and camera
-the way the side mirror dips when reversing to show the kerb
-the ability to change the drivers display to mirror the sat nav screen
-the recognition of speed limits and displaying them in the speedo

-Apple play for music
-puddle lights with Jaguar logo (a gimmick)
-good fuel economy
-Jaguar IPhone App (gives journey records, remote status etc)

Things I don't like so much
-DAB radio - poor signal
-warning sign after two hours of driving- to take a break!
-no heated seats? Unlike 1970's Saabs and the Smart
-higher road tax for £40k +
-glare on screen through glass roof (close blinds)
-complex settings menu
-Lane assist
-parking bleeps
-self park option (too scared to use)
-low profile tyres - a pothole punctured one
-no spare wheel! (See above)

I guess that the dislikes are personal and mostly minor in nature.
Ironically, although this is the most technically advanced and comfortable of all the cars I have owned the 2019 COVID pandemic has severely restricted travel in it. I acknowledge that thus is a minor inconvenience compared with people losing loved ones, livelihoods and suffering health issues so I am not about to com-

plain. We have used it to see parts of Wales that I had not visited for a time and several visits back to Sussex and other places.

As for reliability, both jam related.
One an inconvenience when the electric sun blind on the roof jammed and was replaced under warranty.
A worse problem when the heater fan jammed on a motor 'hot spot' and we had to drive home 80 miles from the airport at night in winter without the heater demisting the window. The mobile mechanic showed me the next day that it could be cured by poking a stick into the motor and pushing the rotor off the spot. I wish I had taken the stick with me to the dealer when they said it was ok - until it happened again and they replaced the whole wiper motor. Still I have learned how to free wiper motors with a stick!

Conclusions

My personal conclusions from fifty years of car ownership? For me and I suspect many others it is a personal, irrational relationship. A lot of people give their cars names - I don't judge the logic of this behaviour, I have just never felt the need to but I do recognise separate personalities in these creations of metal, rubber, plastic and other inert materials. Each has an atmosphere in the cocoon they create around you and the way they behave in response to your control also reveals a particular personality.

I think in this book I may have demonstrated that the choice of one's car is akin to many other personal choices made in your life. Not always purely logical, subject to constraints and sometimes subject to later regret like a fashionable pair of uncomfortable shoes. Considerable expense is often incurred in less time and more limited analysis than when buying a new jacket or coat. Judgements, often inaccurate, are passed on the type of people owning a particular sort of car. I know I do this and I am aware others do too. The manufacturers are very aware of this and often run successful ad campaigns employing techniques to play on this and such campaigns can entirely influence the perception of brands or specific models. I was once introduced to the Ad people who ran the Audi campaign 'Vorsprung durch technik' which apparently means 'progress through technology' but whilst the phrase is well known the translation is not and apparently that's not important -or so the advertising gurus told me. I am unsure about Renault's 'Papa and Nicole campaign'- it always makes me think of 'Allo Allo and Rene and Yvette..so ads may not always hit the target.

What of the future ? I imagine I have bought my last and only second diesel engined car. The next one is very likely to be petrol/hybrid or fully electric. Will I drive a self-driving car - it will take a leap of faith as I am reluctant to use cruise control and don't like the steering correction of 'lane assist' or the 'radar emergency braking' on the Jaguar. Is it likely that electric traction will make car design more anonymous as we have seen to some extent with wind tunnel design. Maybe manufacturers will embrace the opportunity to put exotic bodywork design on standardised electric drive platforms. My wife says she would buy a new Saab 95 estate on an electric platform and an electric VW Split-screen would certainly tempt me. We shall see - there will certainly be exciting developments in the future.

Electric cars aren't just coming - they are here but manufacturers and society will have to crack the problem of range and a comprehensive charging network that can cope with the demands to be placed on it

Production volumes

I thought it might be interesting to see which of our cars were the most popular and also which ones are the rarest but the lack of breakdown within the model ranges has to some extent thwarted that ambition. Here are the production figures that I have been able to glean for some of the cars.
There are some omissions where I just couldn't get figures and gave up in frustration. I imagine Suzuki Vitaras have been produced in hundreds of thousands if not a million plus. At the other end of the scale the Fiat Strada convertible always seemed rare and apparently the DVLA had 9 still taxed in the UK in 2020. The figures quoted are from different sources and differ in their degree of precision from Saab and Triumph measuring to the nearest complete car while others only to the nearest thousand. Saab and Triumph are no longer in business so maybe they were concentrating on the wrong priorities.

MERCEDES C	1993 ON	6900000
FIAT 127	71 - 83	3730000
HONDA JAZZ	2001 ON	3500000
VOLVO 200	74 - 93	2862000
FORD SIERRA	82 - 93	2700000
VW type 2	50 - 67	1900000
SMART FOR 2	98 ON	1500000
JAGUAR XJ	68 - 05	800000
ALFA 156	97 - 05	680000
LR EVOQUE	2011 ON	603000
AUSTIN MON-TEGO	84 - 94	571460
SAAB 96	59 - 78	547221
TRIUMPH HERALD	59 - 71	500000
AUSTIN A35	56 - 68	280897
SAAB 95 est.	59 - 68	110527
TRIUMPH SPITFIRE mk3	67 - 70	65320
VOLVO P1800	61 - 73	39407
TRIUMPH STAG	70 - 77	25939
RENAULT AV-ANTIME	2001 -03	8557
VOLVO 1800 ES	72 - 74	8077
CARABOAT	1973	60

Models of the Cars

The Mini similar to my driving test car and friends Mums cars. The model car industry is quite extensive and over the years I have randomly bought models of our cars when I have seen them. The collection is not yet comprehensive and its not always possible to source them in the right colour. Despite being retired I

still don't have the time or patience to repaint model cars some of which are only a couple of centimetres long.

An Austin A35 - my first car. The bumper and front wheel seem more securely attached to the model than they were on my actual car.

The second car I owned was a Triumph Herald 12/50 similar to this although mine was a dark blue colour with a sunroof and blue vinyl seats.

A Saab 96 saloon. I have never seen a model of the 95 estate so it's either to rare or too ugly to reproduce.
I have found a Saab 96 brochure on Ebay but the £60 price is approaching 20% of what we spent on a whole car!

Suzuki Vitara - hard top

Renault Espace

Volkswagen Type 2 Split screen

Volvo ES - in red not metallic blue

Alfa 156 in the right colour

Mercedes C Coupe

The Avantime

Acquiring a model Smart car was a unique experience as over the years I had bought models of cars we owned or had previously owned. I only had three model cars that we hadn't owned. The Smart was one, the other two are a concept new Splitscreen style VW bus and a 1954 Gullwing Mercedes 300SL. I am not holding my breathe on either of these.

MERCEDES-BENZ

A recent model of the Range Rover Evoque - 3 door here. Ours was the 5 door but the colour is right.

A small Jaguar E-Pace model

A scooter model - not a Vespa but a Lambretta, I think.

Cars in sequence

(Vespa scooter)
Austin A35
Triumph Herald 12/50
Fiat 127
Spitfire Mk 3
Triumph Stag
Jaguar XJ6
Saab 95
Volvo p1800
Volvo 244
Volvo 245 estate
Ford sierra estate
Austin Montego estate
Renault espace
Ford Galaxy
Alfa Romeo 156 2.5
Mercedes c coupe
Mercedes 300 ce
Renault Avantime
Honda Jazz
Range Rover Evoque
Jaguar E-pace

also
Saab 95 green
Saab 96
Fiat Strada convertible
Suzuki Vitara
Honda HRV
Smart car
Caraboat

Brochures

Over the years and latterly on eBay I have accumulated a number of car brochures of the cars we have owned. They are interesting in the variation in styles and the amount of detail they contain. The luxury German cars emphasise the technical details and engineering, Renault tend to be about styling innovation and adaptability and others can be more cryptic and maybe avoiding printing costs ? Any brand with a motor racing investment tries to convince you that your family run about will benefit from their performance in formula one or Le Mans 24 hour race; perhaps they are right. Here is a selection.

SUZUKI
RANGE
VITARA

HONDA
The Honda HR-V 2004

GALAXY
GALAXY

HONDA
The Power of Dreams
Jazz

GALAXY

The Mercedes 230 CE–300 CE-24 Coupés

THE NEW C-CLASS SPORTS COUPÉ

RANGE ROVER EVOQUE
LAND ROVER

NEW JAGUAR E-PACE
JAGUAR
THE ART OF PERFORMANCE

Printed in Great Britain
by Amazon

67931291R00131